Wings of Steel

Wings of Steel

A climber's perspective of the Christian life,
and the story of a world record—
39 continuous days and nights on the side of El Capitan

Richard Jensen

REVIEW AND HERALD® PUBLISHING ASSOCIATION
HAGERSTOWN, MD 21740

All Scripture references are from the *New American Standard Bible*, © The Lockman Foundation 1960, 1962, 1963, 1968, 1971, 1972, 1973, 1975, 1977.

This book was
Edited by Richard W. Coffen
Designed by Bill Kirstein
Cover Design by Helcio Deslandes
Typeset:11.13 /Belwe

PRINTED IN U.S.A.

99 98 97 96 95 94   10 9 8 7 6 5 4 3 2 1

Library of Congress Cataloging in Publication Data
Jensen, Richard, 1959–
    Wings of steel: a climber's perspective of the Christian life,
and the story of a world record—39 continuous days and nights
on the side of El Capitan / Richard Jensen.
        p.   cm.
    1. Rock climbing—California—El Capitan. 2. El Capitan (Calif.)
3. Christian life.
I. Title.
GV199.42.C22E425   1994
796.5′22′79447—dc20   93-11923
                                                       CIP

ISBN 0-8280-0739-X

I dedicate this book to Donna Conant,
my mother, because without her encouragement,
I would never have become a climber.

Acknowledgments

I want to thank Mark Smith. Without him Wings of Steel—this book as well as the climb—would never have gotten off the ground. Not only has he helped in all the phases of this manuscript, but he has also helped me get through the grim moments we have encountered together. Mark has been a true friend in every sense of the word.

Special thanks go to Ann Kominsky for her efforts in unearthing many of the atrocities of sentence structure and punctuation that this manuscript contained.

Many thanks also to Dave Clark ("Super Dave"), Louie Anderson, Dave and Dana Larson, and Jim Kominsky.

What you always read at this point of any book, about how everybody's help is so important to the writer, is not just a sad attempt by the author to portray a false humility. At least in my case, these acknowledgments portray a very real dependence upon the people mentioned above. They have enriched my life.

Finally, I must thank my acquisitions editor, Penny Estes Wheeler. She shatters the notion of the "capricious, unfeeling editor." Penny believed in this manuscript from the beginning, despite the quantity of work that was required to fit it for publication, and spent many hours working with me to make it suitable for the Review and Herald Publishing Association.

Contents

Foreword

In 1992 when Richard Jensen asked me to write a foreword for his forthcoming book *Wings of Steel*, I agreed immediately. As a "formerly famous" climber in Yosemite valley, I've had a certain amount of experience with climbing controversy, and controversy plays a big part in this book, an account of Richard and Mark's experiences on El Capitan and their encounter with the self-proclaimed protectors of climbing in the Yosemite valley. Somehow the resident climbers have come to believe that the walls of Yosemite are their territory and that they are empowered to dictate what is "kosher" and what is not.

I first met Richard sometime in 1982. Actually, it was a chance meeting. Richard and his mother were traveling in Northern California, and they happened to be in Truckee on the same evening that I was presenting a slide show at the Passage.

After the show, Richard, his mother, and I found ourselves talking about his Wings of Steel climb and its attendant controversy. I was rather amazed to learn that this sort of thing was still going on, except that only now it had actually gotten dark and ugly.

Yosemite Valley climbing ethics were invented during the golden age of climbing during the 1960s and has evolved through the years. Some current practices, such as spending a great deal of time "prepping" a route (often so that it can be claimed it was done "all free") and the obsession with free climbing, have led to this rather ludicrous (in my opinion) situation.

But so what? What of all the different tactics of ascent? Are they right or wrong? I think neither. They are merely the result of evolution! Which could lead one to suspect that climbing ethics is not an exact science. However, there are those who take climbing so seriously that they feel they must establish "rights" and "wrongs."

Richard and Mark had set high standards for their Wings of Steel climb. They wanted to push free climbing to their personal limits while at the same time to minimize drilled placements. They even had a good Christian attitude! So who could argue with that? Is it possible that the problem the resident climbers had was more territorial than ideological?

I suspect this might well be the case. After all, Richard and Mark were outsiders. Though quite competent climbers, they had little or no experience in Yosemite Valley. Certainly not of the "in crowd."

Perhaps this could explain the rather atavistic behavior of some of the resident climbersfellows who, mentally, don't appear to be very far removed from the caves! They were simply defending "their" turf.

But enough of this heavy thinking! Enough of this fast foreword! Get on with *Wings of Steel*. It's quite a story!

Warren J. Harding

Preface

From May to July of 1982 a startling story unfolded in Yosemite Valley, California. This valley, a rock climber's Mecca, was the setting for an unprecedented 39-day ascent of the world's largest granite monolith, El Capitan.

This book may appear at first glance to be merely about this world record-setting climb on El Capitan. And, although it is that, it is also about my personal spiritual odyssey on the path of climbing. During the many slide shows I have given on the subject of climbing, and this climb in particular, people are always impressed by one major facet of the program: the many spiritual parallels between climbing and the Christian experience. As time goes on, I see more and more of these. I hope and pray that as you read this book you will see them too. It is my prayer that you will finish this book with a deeper concept of faith, commitment, and God's great love, which will encourage you on your own spiritual path.

Some of the climbing jargon may be a little hard to digest. I have reduced this to a bare minimum. However, climbing is a highly jargonized endeavor. For those who have no climbing background, I have written chapter 1, "Go Climb A Wall," in which I have compiled a climbing crash-course that should have you understanding the basics of big-wall climbing within a few minutes. Much of the jargon is self-explanatory in context.

It will be easy to misunderstand my intent as I write about struggles and victory in the Christian life. Therefore, I wish to make it clear, here at the beginning, that I am a Christian, not a legalist. I believe that only the acceptance of Christ's death on my behalf is needed to effect my salvation. I am saved entirely by what Christ did, and is doing, for me—not by any merit or good works of my own. However, once I accept Christ's death as my own atonement for sin, I have yet to live out my new life in Christ. And this new life requires struggle and effort to accomplish, as anyone who has victories over temptation can affirm. This second aspect is what this book is about. We cannot discuss victorious Christian living until we have established the foundation that Jesus Christ saves us because He is merciful—not because of anything we can do to merit His salvation. Yet, once I am saved and thereby "placed on the climb" so to speak, it still remains for me to climb, albeit in His strength. I am not left static, "saved in my sin" as it were. Far from it! As Ephesians 2:10 says, "For we are His workmanship, created in Christ Jesus for good works." However, anything that I do does not produce a change in God's attitude toward me.

Christ has a climb for each of us. We each have flaws of character and sins that trap us. Yet it is our privilege as Christians to become like Jesus, and He has created a route whereby that is possible. So as we examine the process of victory in Jesus, let's remember that this process does not save us, because salvation is not the result of victory. This process of victory is the natural result of experiencing the salvation Jesus provides. They go hand-in-hand: being saved and becoming Christlike.

Sometimes the climb is hard; sometimes it appears impossible. But we can have faith that Jesus has done the climb, and that He climbs with us. The higher we climb, the more we become like Jesus. The higher we climb, the more we realize that the view alone is worth it!

Go Climb a Wall

You and your partner approach El Capitan on the trail from the meadow. It is a warm—not too hot—day, and you can hear the mosquitoes buzzing all around you. Fortunately, your repellent keeps them at bay so they are little more than a minor intrusion upon your consciousness.

You have more important things to consider as you reach the base of the wall. Panting, you wipe the sweat from your forehead and crane your neck backward, trying to look up the vast sweep of rock. The wall seems impossibly huge, and you wonder if you can make any progress on it. Feeling quite intimidated, you reach out and lightly touch your fingers to the wall. It is cool to your touch, and you press your palm firmly against the expanse of granite.

As you stand there pressing against the wall, your mind calms, seeming to absorb some of the unchanging strength of the rock. You are humbled, sensing a vastness that is overwhelming. Your plans of climbing seem insignificant when you consider your size alongside the towering monolith. An awareness of the ageless, uncaring nature of the rock presses home, and you feel very puny.

Yet the wall is beautiful as it shines in the morning light. It is not unfriendly, merely unconcerned. Whatever progress you make will not matter to it at all. You will come and go; the rock will remain. You want to climb it, to be part of the stream of life that exists upon the wall's giant flank. There is something startlingly attractive about the slab that looms above. You know you will be different for having climbed it. You will be better, calmer, stronger, perhaps purer, because these are the attributes of the wall.

El Capitan, found in Yosemite Valley in central California, defines the term "big wall." Three thousand feet high, El Cap is the world's largest exposed granite cliff and, as such, holds great attraction to wall climbers from around the world. About 60 different routes ascend its flanks, using different features of the cliff. These routes vary from relatively easy to "death routes," where climbers may not return from their efforts. There are few spots left on El Cap where new routes can be forged up the wall. The process of doing such a "first ascent" is a tremendous challenge.

You turn to face your partner, who has been quietly waiting for your mental gymnastics to pass. He is patient. You are both ready to begin, and each of you have different tasks.

You locate your *harness* (Fig. 1) and slip it on like a pair of pants. The front of the harness is formed by a loop of webbing that runs through all three of the main loops and connects them together. This is your tie-in point.

FIG. 1

Having gotten your harness on comfortably, you find the lead end of the rope that your partner has uncoiled into a loose pile on the ground behind you. You tie a *figure 8* knot through the central loop of your harness. The figure 8 knot is strong, non-slip, and easy to untie even after it has been weighted (Fig. 2).

FIG. 2

Harnessed up and connected to the rope, you begin to *rack* gear. The process of racking is different for each climber because each has preferences. However, the object is the same for every climber: get the climbing gear hung on and around the body so that it is as comfortable as possible, organized, and accessible when needed.

The portion of rock you will climb today is a seemingly crackless slab that ascends at about an 80 degree angle. (Ninety degrees is vertical.) The slab is covered with little flakes ranging in size from nickels to silver dollars. Occasionally there are small seams in the rock, which are indented into the wall about the width and depth of a pencil if it were laid on the rock and somehow pressed in. Much longer than a pencil, the seams range in length from about two feet to 10 feet. These flakes and seams are the only features that the slab presents for your upward progress.

You have all the gear needed to utilize these features, and you begin to sort through it. Small loops of cord suspended from your harness are intended for organizing gear around your waist. You also have a couple of padded, two-inch wide slings that hang around your neck and shoulders bandolier-style. You begin to clip pieces of hardware to your waist and shoulder loops.

All the gear you have is clipped together with *carabiners* or *'biners* for short. These 'biners are aluminum links with spring-loaded gates and are used to connect everything to everything else in climbing. Good for about 4,500 pounds, they are strong and light. Each 'biner can hold several pieces of gear (Fig. 3).

As you sort through the gear, you are looking for small items. Although you have gear that will fill up to a five-inch crack, you will only need the smallest placements for this section of the climb. You have several things to select from. There are *copperheads*, which are small blobs of copper on flexible aircraft cable loops. Each of

FIG. 3

these can be pounded into a shallow seam until it is mashed and welded to the sides of the seam. Then a 'biner can be clipped into the cable loop to provide the connection with the wall. The copperheads range in size from #0, which can hold about 500 pounds to #4, which can hold nearly 4,000 pounds. The strength of these placements depends upon the size of the cable and the quality of the mash job in the seam (Fig. 4).

You also have *RURPs* (Fig. 5). RURP is an acronym for "Realized Ultimate Reality Piton." As you finger a RURP, you are impressed with its tiny dimensions. Little bigger than a postage stamp, the RURP has a small blade that can be pounded into very thin and shallow seams. The RURP is threaded with a small cable loop, which is what you will clip a 'biner into. A RURP is as strong as the cable if it is properly pounded into the rock.

FIG. 4

FIG. 5

You also have many *pitons* in your gear pile, but you will not use them for this section of climbing. Pitons are steel spikes with eyes in their ends (Fig. 6). The blade of a piton is pounded into a crack and, once secure, a carabiner is clipped into the eye to make the connection.

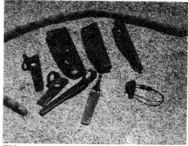

FIG. 6

While the copperheads, or "heads," as they are sometimes called, and the RURPs will get you up any seam, there is a lot of rock in between the seams that offers only tiny flakes as usable features. You have the gear for flakes as well. In your pile of gear are several sizes of *hooks* (Fig. 7). Formed of tempered chrome-molybdenum steel, these hooks are quite strong for their size: 200 to 400 pounds tested strength. A small webbing loop through each hook allows you to clip a 'biner into it. The hooks have points that range in width from 1/16 inch to 1/2 inch for use on different widths of flakes. You take a couple of each size.

The racks of gear you have formed so far are light. You have only about 20 RURPs and 20 copperheads on the sling over your right shoulder; this weighs a little more than a pound. A selection of eight hooks clipped to your waist loop at your left hip weighs about a pound. About 20 'biners are clipped to your harness from your left hip around to your back, which weigh about 5 pounds. On the right hip of your harness you have clipped some webbing loops called *tie-offs* (Fig. 8), which are used for various tasks; these weigh about 1/2 pound. Your rack lacks only one type of hardware.

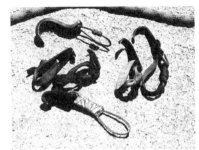

FIG. 7

You can climb seams with RURPs and copperheads and can climb flakes with hooks, but what happens when there are neither seams nor flakes? What about when there are no natural features at all? You have gear for that also.

It is possible, although very time consuming, to drill a hole in blank rock and fill that hole with any one of various *bolts* or *rivets*. Although this is a com-

FIG. 8

pletely unnatural placement, its use is sometimes necessary for upward progress. You don't like to drill the rock, because the whole idea in climbing is to accept the situation that the rock presents naturally and to adapt to it.

This ethic, to use only natural features, is embraced by the climbing community and serves to slow the progress of rock destruction. Because the rock is a limited resource, climbers strive to preserve the climbs in as pristine of a state as possible. Anybody can grab a drill and plant bolts or rivets all the way up a wall, ignoring the natural features that take skill and risk to use. This type of "climbing" is not respected and is avoided. In addition to the ethical consideration, drilling is very hard work.

You are a responsible bolter and plan to use the drill only as a last resort, intending to use the natural features as far as they go. You have a selection of drill bits that includes 1/4-inch, 5/16-inch, and 3/8-inch sizes. The butt end of each bit is tapered to fit into one end of a drill holder, which is also tapered to accept it. A slot in the holder allows insertion of a wedge shaped *drift pin*, which is pounded into the holder when you need to loosen drill bits for removal and replacement (Fig. 9).

FIG. 9

You have a large selection of bolts and rivets for use in different situations. The rivets are 1/4-inch in diameter and about 5/8 inch long. Made of aluminum, they are rather weak, holding approximately 700 pounds. You include two sizes of bolts in your gear pile. The general purpose bolt is 1/4 inch in diameter and about 1 1/4 inches long. It is a split shaft

FIG. 10

of steel that is wider than 1/4 inch at its widest point. As it is pounded into a hole, this split shaft compresses down to 1/4 inch and so provides a springing action to resist pullout. These bolts are quite strong, being good for about 2,000 pounds. You also have 3/8-inch diameter bolts, which are about 2 1/4 inches long. These too are split-shaft steel bolts and can hold about 5,000 pounds. They are used only as anchors because they take nearly 2 hours to place.

Both sizes of bolts have been inserted into *hangers*, which are made of chrome-molybdenum steel (Fig. 10). The bolt hangers provide the connection between the bolt and the 'biner because they have the bolt pounded through one side and a carabiner hole drilled through the other side. You can put about 10 bolts with hangers on a 'biner for the purpose of racking.

The connection between you and a rivet is provided by the *rivet loop*. The rivet loop is merely a small (4 inches in diameter) loop of cable that is looped behind the head of a rivet as the rivet is pounded into the rock. A slide sleeve on the loop can be pulled up close to the head of the rivet to reduce the chance that the loop will wiggle over the head and fall off (Fig. 11).

FIG. 11

You select one 3/8-inch bolt for the anchor, clip a 'biner through its hanger, and clip it to your harness at your back. You clip a small bag containing rivets to your harness as well. You have two drill holders, one containing a 1/4-inch bit for rivets and the other containing a 5/16-inch bit for bolts, and you clip them to the padded gear sling, which hangs from your left shoulder. A small

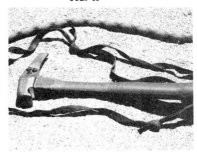

FIG. 12

pouch containing spare bits and a drift pin is clipped to this same gear sling. After clipping to your harness a 'biner with 10 1/4-inch bolts and a 'biner with 15 rivet loops, you are racked up.

Another item needs to be attached to you: your hammer (Fig. 12). Your hammer for wall climbing is a very specialized instrument. Its lightweight graphite and fiberglass handle absorbs vibration and is very resistant to breaking. The head is stainless steel, shaped for pounding in awkward places. The back of the head is grooved and threaded to accept any of several interchangeable picks for pounding different-sized placements. Finally, there is a *save-sling* attached to the handle, which ties into your harness to prevent the hammer from falling out of reach should you drop it.

You admire the design of your hammer as you tie its save-sling into your harness. On the right hip of your harness is a nylon hammer holster into which you insert the handle of the hammer. You're almost ready to climb!

Your gear is racked at different spots on your body for quick and organized deployment. Your hammer rides out of your way in its holster, yet it is within easy reach on your hip. Your harness is comfortable on your hips and supports the weight of gear easily. The rope is tied into the central loop of the harness and runs down between your legs out of the way. Everything seems to be in place.

◆ ◆ ◆

While you have been sorting and racking your gear, your partner has uncoiled another rope, the *haul line*, and has found a good spot to sit and *belay* you. You walk past the haul line, clipping the end of it behind you to your harness, and approach the rock. The haul line will allow you to pull up anything you might need from the ground. Your partner secures himself to the ground by attaching his harness to a sling that he has connected to several good placements (Fig. 13). This *ground anchor* will keep him from being pulled up off the ground by the force of any fall.

FIG. 13

Taking your lead rope, he forms a small loop in it. After forcing this loop through a slot in his *belay plate*, he clips it into a 'biner, which is also clipped to the central loop of his harness (Fig. 14). The rope running through the slot of the belay plate and around the 'biner will provide a great deal

FIG. 14

of friction should you fall, which will enable the belayer to easily hold the rope and stop your fall. The whole process of holding, feeding out, and taking in the rope is called *belaying*, taken from a nautical term that means "to hold."

FIG. 15

FIG. 16

You are *on belay*, tied into a lead rope that is belayed by your partner. You also are racked and tied into a haul line (Fig. 15). You step up to the base of the slab and grab one final item you will need: your *aiders*. The aiders are nothing more than ladders formed from 1-inch flat webbing (Fig. 16). Loops are formed by tying knots in the webbing; these loops provide steps with which to climb up. You have two sets of aiders because while you are standing in one set, you need another set to clip into your next placement. Each set of aiders has loops for both feet so that you can climb up just like on a flexible ladder.

You clip one set of aiders behind you next to the haul line and survey the slab for a line of weakness. Climbing is like playing chess: the more moves you are able to look ahead, the better you can play the game. You stand with both hands pressed against the slab, feeling the unmovable bulk of El Capitan, and contemplate. The ground is level and familiar; the wall is steep and frightening.

The first few placements will have to be hooks until you can reach a 5-foot long seam that is up about 12 feet. After the seam . . . just more hooking. This decided, you look for the best flake. Reaching over your head—no use in picking a placement too close—you feel the flakes in turn. They all feel alike: about as big as quarters glued onto the wall. You caress each one, attempting to feel something—anything that will single out one flake as being better, more attached, than the others. This involves an almost intuitive feel rather than objective knowledge.

One flake seems a little more level than the others. You clip a small *Leeper narrow* hook to your set of aiders and reach up with the hook. The 1/16-inch-wide tip of the hook catches onto the edge of the flake and stays. The aiders hang down from the 'biner almost to the ground (Fig. 17).

The moment has arrived when you must move from the known—the horizontal—into the unknown—the vertical and the insecure. You place one foot into the aiders and apply weight to the hook. As you *weight* the hook, the aiders grow taut, the hook flexes, and the rock creaks a little. Then—slowly—your foot leaves the ground. You are on the hook! It seems to be holding. Your climb has begun.

You move your right foot up one step in the aiders and stand up on it very carefully. Be-

FIG. 17

cause the hook can shift sideways on the flake, it is imperative to keep your weight centered directly below it. After moving your left foot into a loop higher than the right foot and paying close attention to your center of gravity, you move up another loop. As your face moves past the hook, you cover the hook with your hand because if the hook comes off, it might spring back and plant itself in your face.

You place your right foot next to your left foot and pause to reconsider. You are in your *third loops*, so called because they are the third loops down from the 'biner that is clipped into the hook. You are trembling slightly from the mental strain of being supported by such small pieces of rock and metal. You must go on.

You move up another step, into your second loops. As your feet come closer to the hook, it becomes more and more important that you keep them centered directly under the hook. Finally, you gather the courage to top loop. The maneuver to attain your top loops is almost acrobatic, requiring you to place one foot in a top loop, stand up on it—keeping weight centered—then bend at the waist to reach down and help position the other foot in the other top loop (Fig. 18). All this while supported by a a tiny tip of steel on a flake as small as a quarter.

During your top loop machinations, the hook creaked and chipped a little, yet because it still holds you, the climb can go on. You reach up over your head to find another hook flake. The idea is to try to stand on as few hooks as possible—this reduces the number of possible candidates for flake failure—so you reach as high between placements as you can.

Selecting another likely flake, you take your other set of aiders from behind you, clip another Leeper narrow hook into the 'biner,

FIG. 18

and place the hook on the new flake. Taking your right foot out of the top loop in the lower aiders, you place it in the fourth loop of the aiders attached to the higher hook and slowly apply weight. This is the worst part of hooking: being not really on either of the hooks, yet committed to both of them. If the top hook fails, the lower one frequently does too because of your attempts to regain lost balance.

The higher hook creaks and chips yet holds your weight. You move your left foot over into the fourth loop beside the right one and reach down to retrieve your first set of aiders. Plucking the hook off its tiny flake, you pull up your aiders and clip them behind you to your harness. The hook takes up little room in the aider 'biner so you leave it; there will be more hooking to come.

You move up in your aiders, overcome the top looping maneuver, and can just reach the bottom of the 5-foot seam you saw from the ground. This will take a #2 head, so you unclip one from its 'biner, unholster your hammer, and reach both up to the seam. Placing the head into a slight flair in the seam, you use the pick of your hammer to carefully smash the blob of copper into the seam. You must be careful as you pound, because if you miss the copper and hit the cable, it will be damaged and will not hold the weight that it should.

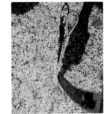

FIG. 19

You mash the blob of copper until, by feel, you can tell that it is flattened into the seam. The cable is not damaged, so the placement should be good for about 1,000 pounds. As you clip your aiders into the loop of the head, you breathe a sigh of relief—well-placed heads rarely pull out, and this seems like a good one (Fig. 19).

Moving onto the head, you grab the lower hook with its aiders and quickly clip them off behind you. Soon you are in your top loops again and can plant another #2 head in the short seam. This head will be right at your chest level because the seam ends and you want to get the head in before moving back onto hooks. Having two heads in the seam is much more secure than having only one.

Once the second head is placed, you clip aiders into it and then reach down to your ankles and clip the lead rope through the 'biner that is clipped into the lower head. This connects the rope to the rock, indirectly, through the cable of the copperhead, the head of which is melded to the rock. It is your first protection placement.

As you are climbing, there are two kinds of placements: those that the rope runs through (protection) and those that the rope does not run through (temporary). Hooks are examples of temporary placements, so called because they are connected with the rock only long enough to move you a little higher, at which time they are removed and reused higher up.

The reason hooks are not generally used for protection is that they are not strong enough to hold falls and so are not worth the effort to secure in place as you go past them. There are large hooks, called *claws*, which are sometimes taped to the wall for security and used as protection. These claws are good for approximately

800 pounds and so are substantially stronger than the smaller hooks. Some desperate situations arise when even a hook is better than nothing, and the climber may waste time trying to hang gear on the hook to weight it, attempting to secure it on the wall. This is generally futile as the hook will straighten out under the force of a fall. However, climbers rely on psychological protection sometimes.

The copperheads you have in the seam, though, are good and would hold short falls, so you clip the rope into them as you move up. The hooking has begun again, because nothing is visible above except tiny flakes.

After moving up onto several hooks—with great trepidation—you come to a blank spot. You find no flakes, seams, or other features within reach in any direction. You will have to use a drilled placement. You consider your position (you are up about 30 feet off the ground) and decide that you should place a bolt instead of a rivet because you want a protection placement that will positively hold any fall. You don't want to rip past it and hit the ground.

Considering that you have used seven natural placements so far, you are not concerned about the use of a drilled, unnatural placement at this point. Your code of ethics deems this an acceptable drilling ratio for the blank slab. You reach for the drill and hammer.

Because you are top-looped on a hook, it is important that you stay very still as you drill. Any attempt to shift your feet or legs will change your center of gravity, probably cause the hook to shift and pop off the flake, and send you plummeting. Because you are about 15 feet above the top copperhead, you are assured of a 30-foot fall if your hook should fail.

The leader on a climb takes the risks and will always fall double the distance of the rope run out between him and the placement that catches him (Fig. 20). Because you are only 30 feet off the ground, if the hook you are on fails, you will ground out—unless your belayer is very good and can pull some rope through his plate as you fall. If he can do this, it will shorten the working length of the rope and, thereby, the total fall distance. Even if he can do this for

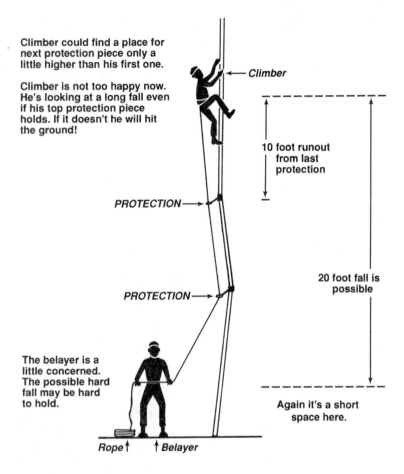

Climber could find a place for next protection piece only a little higher than his first one.

Climber is not too happy now. He's looking at a long fall even if his top protection piece holds. If it doesn't he will hit the ground!

Climber

10 foot runout from last protection

PROTECTION

PROTECTION

20 foot fall is possible

The belayer is a little concerned. The possible hard fall may be hard to hold.

Again it's a short space here.

Rope↑   ↑ *Belayer*

FIG. 20

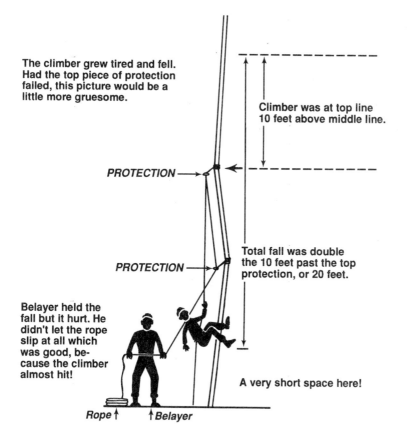

The climber grew tired and fell. Had the top piece of protection failed, this picture would be a little more gruesome.

Climber was at top line 10 feet above middle line.

PROTECTION →

Total fall was double the 10 feet past the top protection, or 20 feet.

PROTECTION →

Belayer held the fall but it hurt. He didn't let the rope slip at all which was good, because the climber almost hit!

A very short space here!

Rope ↑   ↑Belayer

you, the top copperhead must hold. If it fails under the impact of the fall (which can reach as much as 3,000 pounds for a 170-pound climber), the fall will be lengthened by another 10 feet, because the second head is 5 feet below the top one, and you will ground out for sure—no matter how good your belayer is. As you drill, looking down, terra looks most firma!

FIG. 21

Drilling is a long, slow process accomplished by pounding on the end of the drill holder opposite the bit, which is against the wall, and turning the holder slowly to keep the bit's tip biting into new rock deeper in the hole (Fig. 21). After pounding and turning for a few moments, you must remove the bit from the wall, reach up with your lips, and blow the accumulated rock dust from the hole. Then the drill goes back into the ever deepening hole, and the pounding and turning continue.

After a half hour of work—in terror of the hook failing—you pound the bolt in. Clipping aiders into the eye of the hanger, you romp right up on them to rest. The half hour of motionlessness has left your legs cramped, your feet asleep, and your arches bruised. Resting on the bolt, you realize that it has taken you hours to cover the last 30 feet of rock, yet the climb has only begun!

All too soon you realize that you must continue. Top-looping the bolt, you find another hook flake, and you're climbing again.

Many hook flakes, copperhead seams, rivets, and a few bolts later, you have run out about 145 feet of lead rope. Because modern climbing ropes are either 150 or 165 feet long, you decide to set up an anchor. You want those who use 150-foot ropes to be able to follow your leads even though you prefer to use 165-foot ropes. That extra 15 feet has helped you out more than once.

◆ ◆ ◆

The term *pitch* is used to describe the length of climbing that takes place between two anchors. Your first anchor was at the ground where your belayer is clipped into the ground anchor.

Because this will be another anchor, you have just climbed the first pitch of the route: 145 feet long.

A belay anchor on the wall must be *bomb proof!* This means that redundancy is in order. You must succeed in placing enough strong protection placements close to each other so that they can all be slung together with webbing slings to form an anchor that cannot be pulled from the wall under any conceivable force. Both of you will hang from this anchor, and the leader may fall past it from higher up. If the anchor pulls out of the wall, you will both fall 145 feet to the inevitable "splat." Your job is to see that this cannot happen.

Since the anchor will be placed on blank rock (no seams or cracks; a hook is not an anchor placement), a group of bolts is the only option you have. Two 1/4-inch bolts and one 3/8-inch bolt constitute a bomb-proof anchor, and you begin to place them.

You place a 1/4-inch bolt to the left of your reach, a 1/4-inch bolt to the right of your reach, and the 3/8-inch bolt in the middle. The three bolts are in a line, and you sling them all together with very strong 1-inch tubular webbing, which is good for 4,000 pounds. All the webbing is doubled to prevent the possibility of a bad piece causing disaster.

Once the bolts are in and slung together, you pull up some of your lead rope, tie a figure 8 knot, and clip it into the anchor. This connects your harness to the anchor while at the same time anchoring the lead

FIG. 22

rope for the *clean.* Next you pull up some haul line, tie it into a figure 8 knot, and clip it into the anchor. Surveying the anchor, you yell down that you are *off belay*—the ropes are anchored, and the clean can begin. Your partner, who is now finished belaying, will be connected to two independent ropes as he comes up. This precludes a single rope cutting over an unseen edge and causing certain death.

Your partner approaches the base of the pitch with a set of

jumars in his hands. The word "jumar" can be used either as a noun or as a verb depending upon its application. A jumar is a device that, once attached to the rope, will slide up the rope but not down (Fig. 22). This allows the cleaner to ascend rapidly an anchored rope by sliding one jumar up, weighting it with an aider, sliding the other jumar up, then weighting it, while sliding the first jumar higher, and so on. This process is jumarring. The jumars not only allow the cleaner to ascend—stopping at will to remove placements—but also attach him to the rope through slings to his harness, providing a passive belay. Because three points of attachment to the rope are deemed necessary, the cleaner also attaches himself to another line, which is also anchored above, with a *Gibbs ascender*. Similar to a jumar, a Gibbs will slide up the rope but not down. As the cleaner ascends the ropes, the Gibbs follows him faithfully up the haul line, requiring no effort to provide the third point of attachment to the rock through the second rope.

Your partner attaches the two jumars and the Gibbs to the proper ropes and jumars quickly up to your first copperhead, the first protection placement, and after attaching his hammer to it, jerks madly with his hammer until the head pulls loose from the seam.

Reaching the next head, he repeats the process, leaving the seam clean for any other party of climbers who might wish to do your route. They can exercise the skill of making their own placements in the seam.

Your partner jumars up to your first bolt and has gained the first 30 feet of climbing in minutes what took you hours to negotiate. Leading is truly the risky, time-consuming part of the climb, whereas cleaning is merely monotonous. After unclipping the lead rope from the 'biner and unclipping the 'biner from the bolt hanger, your partner clips this 'biner to a rack and moves on. All drilled placements are left in the wall so other climbers can use them on future ascents.

The clean proceeds quickly: the heads and RURPs are jerked or pried from their seams, 'biners are unclipped from bolts and rivets, and hooking sections are jumarred past. Soon your partner arrives at the anchor. The sun is almost set—perfect timing—and a perfect day of climbing is almost over. All that remains is to return to the ground and hike out for the night.

Using your belay plate for friction, you *rappel* down the ropes to the ground. Once you reach the ground, your partner rappels down, and you hide all your gear in the forest, where you can find it for the next day's climbing.

Returning to the base of the wall, you look up again. This time you do not have such a feeling of intimidation. The day of climbing has made you feel like you belong—you feel closer to the wall. The sight of the ropes hanging from the anchor, 145 feet above, fills you with joy. The first pitch is *fixed*, so you can quickly jumar back to your high point with little effort and no risk. The next lead is your partner's, so you are through with the risk for a while. Both of you are pleased with the day's climbing and hope that the next pitch will go as well.

That is the way walls are climbed: one pitch at a time. The work and risk load is divided between the climbers and must be confronted a little at a time. If one looks at the whole huge wall in one chunk, discouragement—almost despair—sets in. You must maintain your focus on the section of climb you presently confront. Nothing else really matters, because unless that section is properly handled, there will be no need to consider anything higher up—you will never reach it. So, the climb consists of one placement after another. Each placement embraces the essence of the whole climb.

The climbing described so far in this chapter is called *direct aid* climbing or simply "aid" for short. In aid climbing, the climber relies entirely upon the gear for upward progress. One is actually climbing on the gear, and so the quality of the placements one uses determines the difficulty of the pitch. All pitches are *rated* or appraised according to the hardest section a climber will encounter. Aid ratings are always in a certain state of flux, yet there are basically five main grades of aid climbing.

A1 simply implies the easiest, most secure aid climbing that can be found. An A1 pitch might be a *bolt ladder*, where every placement is a 2,000-pound-test bolt, or a deep crack into which one bomb-proof placement after another can be seated. A1 implies that the leader will not fall because every aid placement is too strong to fail. Even if, by some quirk, a placement did fail, the next placement below would positively hold the fall. So A1 means no risk and generally quick climbing.

All other aid ratings are determined primarily by the potential distance the leader could fall from the worst spot on the pitch. Although other factors can play a part in the rating (for example, a fall that would result in the leader hitting a ledge or other object), the fall distance is the important point. Following is a brief description of A2 through A5.

A2: The leader faces a fall of up to 15 feet. If a placement fails, one or two others might fail under the impact. However, at least the third placement down will catch. The risk of hitting something during the fall is not a factor.

A3: The leader faces a fall of up to 25 feet. If a placement fails, two to four others might fail under the impact. However, at least the fourth placement down will catch. The risk of hitting something during the fall may be a factor.

A3 +: The leader faces a fall of up to 30 feet, or a shorter fall in which hitting something becomes a consideration. This will generally result in some personal injury.

A4: The leader faces a fall of up to 40 feet, or could hit something in a shorter fall. The difference between A3 + and A4 is very subjective and reflects a greater feeling of fear and risk.

A4 +: The leader faces a fall of up to 50 feet, or probably will hit something while on the way down the full 50-foot fall. A4 + generally denotes a serious risk of injury or death.

A5: The leader faces a fall longer than 50 feet and probably will hit something while in flight. The A5 rating implies enormous risk of serious injury or death.

The ratings beyond A1 involve the tendency that weak placements have to *zip* out of the wall under impact. Jerking multiple placements loose during a fall is jokingly called a *zipper fall*. There is a climb in Yosemite called "Jack the Zipper," which is rated A4 +. Climbers tend to snicker morbidly about such climbs, yet they climb them.

There is another kind of climbing that is done on big walls. Whereas "aid" climbing is accomplished by climbing on the gear, "free" climbing is done by never weighting the gear at all. The protection placements still exist and the rope runs through them, yet the leader does not use them at all for upward progress. The gear is only used for protection in the event of a fall, all upward progress must be made by the climber relying only on his body's ability to cling to the rock.

Free climbing is a completely different game than aid climbing and, as such, has its own rules, ratings, and ethics. If a climber is doing a free section and, about to fall, grabs a placement to keep from falling, the pitch is no longer free. That climber is back in the realm of aid climbing and can no longer claim a free ascent of the pitch. Climbers take this ethic very seriously and, in general, the honor system works very well.

Free climbing has become a more popular part of the sport than aid climbing. Perhaps this is because free climbing is less of an engineering project and more of a gymnastic endeavor than is aid climbing. Whatever the attraction for each climber, everyone who free climbs has some desire to be able to free climb harder and harder pitches. To succeed at this, most climbers participate in some form of physical training to build up weak areas of their bodies.

Free climbing is rated in a completely different manner than aid climbing. While aid ratings are dependent upon relatively objective fall potentials, free ratings are dependent upon a purely subjective feeling of difficulty that arises from trying to get one's body up a particular pitch without resorting to aid. It is assumed in a free rating that protection is adequate for safety, and protection is not a factor in the rating at all.

Of course, a pitch may have a reputation as being unprotectable, in which case, if you are interested in the climb, you had better know that the pitch is well within your free climbing limits.

On such a pitch you had best not fall, or you may take the equivalent of an A5 fall. Mental and physical control is the essence here.

Because free ratings are purely subjective, before a new free climb can be rated, many people have to do the climb in order to get a consensus rating from all of them. Since free climbing is a physically strenuous form of climbing, you may find yourself unable to do a climb that should have been within your ability if, for example, you were up late the night before, feel a little sick, or any number of other subjective factors are at work. With this in mind, let's examine a synopsis of the free climbing ratings. The percentage of climbers who are able to attain a particular standard of class 5 free climbing will follow.

Class 1—Walking. No rope is needed. This has not yet entered the realm of climbing.

Class 2—Hiking. No rope is needed although the trail may be steep and slippery in spots. This is not climbing yet.

Class 3—Scrambling. No rope is needed, although the hike may involve using hands as well as feet. There is no real exposure to a fall potential yet, so this is not climbing.

Class 4—Scrambling. A rope may be needed for beginners because the scrambling involves hands as well as feet. Although there is a certain exposure to a fall potential, this is not yet considered climbing.

Class 5—Climbing. A rope and protection are needed to protect the leader. There is exposure to a fall potential, and any fall must be stopped by the rope and protection. This class is broken into at least 14 categories ranging from 5.0 to 5.14, with the grades of 5.10 and above also having a letter sub-grade of a,b,c, or d.

Because the lowest rating in free climbing is 5.0, any climber must be able to climb 5.0. Therefore, 100 percent of modern climbers can climb 5.0 pitches. This is to be compared with only about 5 percent of climbers who can climb 5.11 and only about .1 percent of climbers who can climb 5.14. Obviously, the larger of a number following the 5.0, the more severe the climbing.

Like the aid climber, who has special tools such as aiders and jumars to help him, the free climber has tools. These tools include special shoes, which resemble high-top basketball shoes and have

a smooth, very soft rubber sole for improved friction on the rock (Fig. 23). Another tool for hard climbs is gymnastic chalk. The chalk is powdered then put into a small bag with a drawstring closed top: a chalk bag. The bag is attached to the climber in some convenient spot so that sweaty hands can reach the "magic" white pow-

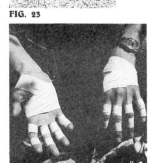

FIG. 23

FIG. 24

FIG. 25

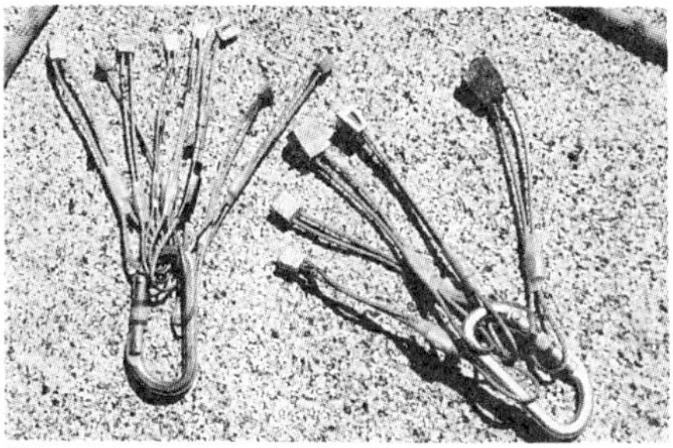

FIG. 26

FIG. 27

der (Fig. 24). The chalk helps dry the sweat from nervous and exerted hands to provide a more secure grip. Some barefoot free climbers even chalk their feet. Wide adhesive tape is also used to help the climber avoid the need for skin grafts. Wrapped around those areas that will be in contact with the rock, the tape acts as a second skin, preserving that of the climber for future climbs (Fig. 25).

The protection on free climbs may consist of any piece of hardware that the aid climber might use. In addition to the RURPs, copperheads, pitons, claws, and drilling gear that we have already covered, the climber also has strange *nuts* at his disposal. The term "nut" is used to describe any piece of gear that is not placed with a hammer. Even a piton can be a nut if it is not hammered into place.

Nuts come in all shapes and sizes. These include *stoppers* (Fig. 26), which are wedge-shaped nuts, the intent of which is to jam in a narrow spot in a crack. There are also *hexentrics* or *hexes* (Fig. 27), which are six-sided nuts, turned in a crack so that two flats catch and cam in harder as weight is applied. Then there are *cams*, both passive and active. Passive cams are so called because the weight of the climber or the force of a fall causes them to tighten in the crack. Active cams are designed so that a spring provides the active force that secures the cam in the crack. These also lock into the crack harder as more force is applied to them.

FIG. 28

An active cam is more secure in the crack than a passive cam simply because a passive cam requires external force just to stay in place, whereas an active cam supplies that force by virtue of its design. Passive cams come under many names. A hex can be a passive cam and there are also *camlocks* and *tri-cams* (Fig. 28). There are many kinds of active cams on the market today, although all are take-offs on the original: the

FIG. 29

friend (Fig. 29). The friend is truly friendly to the desperate climber, who can quickly shove it into a crack and have it expand to fill that crack, providing instant protection. There is generally little effort in placing a friend, for they come in many sizes and fit a broad range of cracks.

All nuts may also be used in aid climbing. The only real difference between aid and free climbing is that on aid you are climbing on the gear, while free, you never weight the gear. This is primarily a stylistic distinction, serving no real purpose regarding actually getting up a wall. It is simply acknowledged that a climber should try to climb free as far as possible, then use aid. However, often the hardest aid climbs are more mentally traumatic than the hardest free climbs. So going onto aid does not guarantee easy climbing.

As you have begun to guess, style plays an important role in other climbers' judgment of a given climb. It is not merely enough to get up a climb; one must climb in the best possible style. For example, if a climb were done free on the first ascent, it is subsequently considered to be bad style for another party to do the route using aid. The fact that the second party also climbed the route is meaningless because it did not match the standard set by the first ascent party.

Needless to say, the responsibility involved in putting up a new route is tremendous because the first ascent party is expected to be experienced and qualified enough to put up the new route using the best possible modern style. If style were not important to climbers, anybody could get up anything using the drill and nothing more. Although there would be no risk, no skill, no attempt to cope with the existing features of the rock, the bolt ladder would be considered a valid climb if the only issue was getting up.

◆ ◆ ◆

Whereas mountain climbing focuses upon reaching the summit, rock climbing is far more concerned about *how* one reaches the summit. Without good style, one might as well hike a trail to the top because one is not really "climbing" anyway. It is more important how one climbs than that he climbs.

Part of big wall climbing is the fact that it takes multiple days to get up the wall. Because of this fact there is a strong temptation to *siege climb* the wall. Sieging is the term applied to the process of fixing pitches higher and higher until one is almost up the wall yet has never committed to living on the wall. The siege climber spends every night back on the ground, after fixing ropes a little higher during the day, and can enjoy all the comforts of home despite the supposed "fact" of "climbing" the wall.

Different degrees of sieging are allowable, depending upon the length and difficulty of a given route. If the route in question normally takes only about five days to ascend, it is bad style to fix half of it. However, if the route might take two weeks to climb, people are seen to fix anywhere from 1/3 to 1/2 of the route before they haul all the necessities off the ground and go for the final push. Going for the final push simply means that the climbers are independent from the ground and from other climbers until they reach the rim. Self-sustained and having everything they need, they live on the wall as they climb.

FIG. 30

But how do you sleep? Very simply and comfortably! You have a *portaledge* (Fig. 30), which is similar to a collapsible army cot suspended by slings. For bad weather you have a tentlike *rain fly* or simply *fly* that covers the whole portaledge, keeping weather on the outside.

How do you eat? All food and water is hauled up in large bags called, surprisingly enough, *haul bags*. The same holds true of everything you might need during the course of your chosen climb. If the climb might take five days, you would bring five days' worth of necessities in a haul bag. The bags are hauled after each pitch is led and a higher anchor is established. Interestingly enough, the jumars are an integral part of the hauling setup, because if a jumar is hung upside down, it will let rope slide up through it, but not back down. So, as rope is hauled up, the hauler can rest while the jumar holds the rope without allowing it to slide back down. Using the right hauling techniques, one can haul more than one's own body weight.

At night on the wall, after the climbing is done and the bags are hauled, you set up your portaledge and possibly the rain fly as well. You then anchor a length of rope long enough to reach from the anchor down to your portaledge. After tying into that length of rope, you are anchored to retreat down to the portaledge for the night.

The climber might have a piece of 2-inch-wide tubular webbing wrapped several times around the waist and knotted. This webbing loop is called a *swami belt* and allows the climber to remove harness and/or pants without ever untying from the anchored rope. On the wall, the climber is never untied from an anchored rope. One is either tied in to a harness or swami or both for the duration of the wall climb.

What if you get in trouble on the wall? Can you be rescued if you get hurt? A rescue team is headquartered in Yosemite Valley. *Rescue Site* is the term used to identify the members of the Yosemite rescue team, who reside in a special campsite in Camp 4 (also called Sunnyside Campground). This group—the rescue team who live at Rescue Site—are an elite group of climbers with extensive Yosemite climbing background. For this reason, they are given the task of rescuing woebegone climbers from the sides of Yosemite's massive walls.

Now, they get paid to do this work, as they rightly should. As you can imagine, lowering over the rim of a 3,000-foot cliff to get help to a stranded or injured climber is a demanding way to make a buck. Some would-be rescuers have ended up worse off than the person for whom the rescue was initiated.

It is a real honor to be considered a skilled enough climber to join the rescue team. Their lot is one of great prestige, if not security. So, many people do climbs in the valley with one purpose being that of making an impression on the right people, thereby to be considered for membership in the team.

In addition to the prestige and pay, the rescue team enjoys free camping and an unlimited stay privilege. Whereas everyone else pays to stay in Camp 4, those at Rescue Site pay nothing. Whereas everyone else has a maximum stay limit of one week during peak season and a month during off season, those at Rescue Site stay indefinitely.

This is all fine and good. The rescue team does good work, and the members enjoy privileges and pay. A problem can occur when the rescue team members begin to feel that they own the valley, that they have special rights to it, that they are superior climbers and so can dictate what another person has the right to do in "their" valley. The fact of this attitude problem becomes apparent as the story of *Wings of Steel* unfolds.

CHAPTER 2

Beginnings, the Call to Climb

I remember clearly when I first realized what climbing was all about. It was during the summer of 1969 at a camp in the woods, a place where kids go to experience something new and learn something exciting. Classes are offered, the intent of which is to plant a seed of interest in some hobby or skill that will perhaps blossom into full-fledged ability in the chosen area.

I chose archery. With thoughts of Robin Hood, I dreamed of being able to pull the bow back, let fly with the arrow, and sink it with deadly accuracy into any target. I knew what I wanted long before the bus deposited me and many others onto the camp premises. This, however, was the only thing that I did know. I did not know anyone else in the bus or at the camp. I did not know which cabin I was to sleep in. I did not know whether or not I would be accepted or liked. I did not know what being away from home for a week would be like. Heavy questions for a 10-year-old mind.

When the bus got to camp and we all piled off, the first fear factor was to find the right line in which to register myself for my chosen class. So many people and such a big place! Finally, with the help of a camp counselor, I found the archery "line." Surprise—no line! I stepped up to the table only to find that my class was full and therefore closed. Now I had no clue of what to do except locate another counselor to help me find another class to register into. This, I realized, was very important, as all the kids in a class slept together in one cabin with their counselors. No class, no cabin!

With frightful thoughts in my mind, I stood alone in a clearing. A friendly fellow came over and offered to help me out. (At least those who ran the camp had enough foresight to hire a good ratio of counselors to kids.) He explained that most of the classes were closed—except rock climbing.

Rock climbing? To my young and very petrified mind, this was as bad as a class in jumping off a bridge. Unfortunately, it was a choice between that and bead work, which was a double cabin, coed class. I was more frightened of girls than of jumping off a bridge, so . . .

The next morning after breakfast, I found myself with about 15 other kids and our two counselors hiking through the underbrush toward our goal: a 50-foot cliff, which our counselors had the stupidity to tell us was called "The Claw."

Just the mention of the word "Claw" sent ripples up my spine. I had no idea, as we walked, just what form of torture would beset us when we reached The Claw. But I was sure that I would be unable to cope with it.

They called it "rappelling," which they said was a climbing term for sliding down a rope in order to get from the top of the climb back to the ground. Then I realized I was doomed. We would be forced to be airborne for no conceivable reason other than to get back to the ground. Why not simply stay on the ground in the first place? Suddenly bead work seemed terribly inviting! I had the feeling that the girls would probably not kill me as quickly as rappelling off The Claw would.

As we hiked along, I pulled up next to one of our counselors and asked, "Is bead work still open?" This revelation of fear brought forth peals of laughter from my peers and a slow smile from the man I was talking to. He explained that all the classes were closed and that I was stuck with rock climbing. Oh well, everybody has a bad day sometimes!

Then the counselor pulled me to the back of the group and began to explain that he and his friend did not delight in terrorizing little kids and that rock climbing was really a wonderful thing. I replied that hanging in the air didn't seem wonderful to me at all.

At this point he stopped the whole group and began talking to us. We were all encouraged to express our fears and get them explained. He told us why he was a climber and why he enjoyed teaching climbing. Then his partner did the same thing.

During the course of that hour I didn't ever feel the wonder and power of what they were describing, but two very important things did happen. I began to *want* to climb and I began to trust these two men with my life, a privilege that had been previously extended only to my mother. It seemed that some of the apron strings were about to be cut.

After the discussion, we continued to hike until The Claw came into view, but I was high enough on trust not to feel the fear yet. When we reached the top of The Claw by the back way, I stayed a long way from the edge of the drop. I began to feel the dizziness of height just sitting there and watching the two counselors uncoil the ropes.

As we gathered in a circle on top of the rock, the counselors showed us the equipment we would be using. We got our first introduction to harnesses, slings, ropes, and carabiners.

My confidence grew as they fastened onto my harness a couple of carabiners. Harnessed up, I examined the carabiners. They were small and clean and lightweight. I liked them. My trust increased.

Next the counselors showed us the pitons and pounded a few into some convenient cracks in the top of The Claw. Using a process that I didn't understand, they clipped the ropes into all four or five carabiners, which were also clipped into the driven pitons.

With the ends of two ropes thus connected to the rock in this indirect fashion, the men threw the rest of the two ropes over the edge. The ropes seemed to fall a long time before they hit the ground.

The counselors connected each of the other kids to one of the ropes one by one, and the kids slid over the edge and out of sight. I carefully positioned myself to remain last in line. I was again certain that I wanted no part of this activity as I heard the sounds of grunting, clanking, and scraping coming up from the depths. Visions of horror filled my mind: small bodies lying crushed and bottom, little spatters of blood on the rock, bones poking out, torn flesh . . .

"Ricky, come on, it's you're turn." The counselor had my number. We were alone on the top of The Claw.

I wanted to run but was too dizzy. "No, I can't. I don't want to go over. I'm afraid of heights—of falling. I don't know what's down there. I won't lean back that way, the ropes won't hold me, and I'm . . ."

"Hold it, hold it," the counselor could sound soothing when necessary. "I want you just to look over the edge—just look over."

With great apprehension, I looked over. No little bodies, no blood or gore, just a long drop. The rock seemed clean and innocent of any crime. The others were well and happy. I sat in thought as the counselor sent the others back to camp with the first counselor. Suddenly it didn't seem so bad. It had worked for everybody else. Why not for me? They had even seemed to enjoy it.

The counselor, who I found out was also named Rick, explained again how to lean back to keep my feet against the rock and sort of sit in the air, supported by the ropes. He told me how to let rope slowly slide through my hand into the friction brake on my harness, which would lower me down the rope. Simple principle. It could work!

Suddenly I was at the edge, clipped in and leaning back slightly, supported by the ropes and my harness. My eyes were locked with Rick's, my salvation, although he couldn't really do anything.

Then he told me to lean back some more and let out a little rope. His voice was calm, unconcerned—this was commonplace for him. I let out some rope and jerked downward. Fear paralyzed me, and I tried to think of a way to get back onto the top. Then I realized that I couldn't. The two-foot distance that I had slid down was an insurmountable barrier to safety. I was trapped in the vertical. As I fully understood my predicament two things happened: I became resigned to my fate and so my fear lessened, and I saw that I could still go down one way or another and end up on the ground.

Hope! Despite being in the most scary spot of my life, I could get out of it. I released some more rope and, accordingly, slid down a little. Release rope and slide, release rope and slide. It took on a warped familiarity. I began to feel in control of the situation. The ropes held, the brake worked, my feet were on the rock, and it was like walking down backward. I felt less afraid.

It took me a long time to reach the ground, but by the time I had, I felt confident that this was not the quick way to die that I had thought it was.

Rick told me to unclip from the ropes and come back up to the top. By the time I arrived I had stopped most of the subconscious jitters that had plagued me all day. Then I saw that the ropes were still anchored to the pitons. Here we go again!

The second time I was not nearly as scared. Not only did I trust Rick, I trusted the rappelling system as well. Over the edge I went. This time Rick had me bounce away from the wall on the way down. Springing away from the rock with my feet, I began to see it as a challenge conquered, a fear overcome.

When I got back to the top, we readied the gear so that we could return to camp. As we coiled the ropes we talked about my feelings, and the whole strange event began to seem real and normal instead of like some nightmare.

The rest of my days at camp were like that. Every day we all would go out together to do some simple climb or to rappel again. Then Rick and I would return alone later. I never showed any potential as a climber. I was always the most afraid of each new experience and the most unable to cope with it. Rick always showed great patience and did wonders for my fears and doubts as I trusted him. Yet, while I learned how to tie knots and make harnesses and other memory-dependent tasks, I never got any good at climbing itself.

I remember being pulled up out of a body-sized crack from above. Climbing the large crack was called "chimneying" because the struggles resembled what you would have to do if you ever needed to get up the inside of a real chimney. I was completely exhausted by my efforts to make progress in the crack. As I was hoisted out of it, I thought about the fact that no one else had climbed it because they were working on much harder things over to the right somewhere.

On the last day of camp, just before we piled back into the buses, Rick explained to me that some people were natural climbers whereas others just weren't cut out for it. He was talking about coordination, mental frame, and some other things that I couldn't understand. I saw then that I was limited by something which I couldn't define or understand, and I was very unsettled by this realization. At that moment I began to want to be a climber, a real climber. I wanted to dissolve my limitations, at least to define or understand them.

When I returned home, I struggled to understand why I couldn't climb. Not finding any answers, one thing seemed clear: To be a climber, one must climb. Because there were no rocks, equipment, or partners at my disposal, I sought out trees. The eucalyptus trees at the park became my second home. Towering more than 100 feet high, they seemed challenging enough.

There followed a few years during which I climbed only trees. I got to enjoy the feeling of being as high as the birds, completely removed from the mundane world and above all normal problems. As I grew older, friends would offer me different drugs that they seemed to enjoy, but they held no attraction for me. Being high in the trees, swayed by the wind on the tip-top tiniest limbs, was drug enough for me. My friends, of course, had no interest in following me up to the heights.

During those years I developed coordination, strength, and confidence. Then I met Gary, who also had an interest in climbing. Both being poor, we manufactured harnesses out of our cotton karate belts. We used cheap braided water-ski rope to rappel on, and even used padlocks as carabiners.

We would climb high into a tree, anchor our ski ropes to a strong branch, gird ourselves in our karate belts, wrap the ropes a few times around the locks for friction, and connect them to our harnesses. Once the locks were locked to our harnesses, we would hop off our branches and slide down to the ground.

We loved it. Only years later did I realize what ignorant fools we had been. I remember laughing at Gary because one day he couldn't remember the combination to his lock once he had reached the ground. After that we switched to key locks.

Slowly I learned. I checked out every climbing book from every library in my area and began to grasp the principles involved. My mother gradually bought me different kinds of gear and encouraged me to continue my efforts. With my meager collection of gear, Gary and I broadened our scope of climbs until we were actually climbing at a somewhat respectable level. We visited established climbing areas and learned about new techniques and ratings. We learned "aid climbing" and enjoyed it immensely.

So, I progressed. Only now, looking back, can I understand what I lacked at summer camp and took years to gain: a willingness to confront and cope with whatever God should decide to put in my pathway, while trusting Him to have my best interest uppermost in mind. I had spent my childhood looking for the most comfortable, easy way. I had been a quitter. I learned that climbers don't quit.

◆ ◆ ◆

One thing set me on the new path of climbing. I realized that I lacked something very important to me and I didn't know where to find it. I realized that I was deeply flawed, and needed to get corrected somehow.

As I was realizing this fact, Rick continued to be patient and kind to me. Had he not, I would have been overwhelmed, browbeaten, and probably would have lost my desire to continue my self-confrontation. Thank God for Rick's accepting attitude and tact. I was able to confront my weakness, without despair. A deep desire to be different motivated me to change.

The first step in my Christian life was to understand that I am deeply flawed, weak, and unable to make myself what I should be. No matter how good a life I lead, when compared to the matchless life of Jesus Christ and His perfect self-control, my life is a shambles. Weakness, lack of control, and lack of true love come through at every turn of the road. Without Christ my life is bent on self-gratification and comfort-seeking, even though I might try to fool myself into thinking that I am a "good" person.

Non-Christians are unable to see or even imagine this reality because of the standard to which they compare themselves. Only when compared with the law of God, as evidenced in the life of Christ, can we see ourselves as we really are. We must not look into the wrong mirror, or we will be deceived.

It was hard, and still is, to confront this fact. I must see myself as only God sees me, and like Paul to realize that "I know that nothing good dwells in me" (Rom. 7:18). But once I feel the despair Paul felt as he cried out, "Wretched man that I am! Who will set me free from the body of this death?" (verse 24). I can truly appreciate the next saving verse, "Thanks be to God." It has been accomplished "through Jesus Christ our Lord!" (verse 25).

This is the essence of my climb: seeing myself as helpless without Jesus and laying hold on His mighty arm as my only strength.

All who do this will be lifted out of the pit and established on the Rock. Once your feet are on the Rock, the climb can begin, the climb toward the character of Christ!

CHAPTER 3

◆

Counting the Cost

Eventually I stood in El Capitan Meadows and looked up at the biggest monolith of granite in the world: 3,000 feet tall and more than a mile and a half wide. I could not imagine what it would take to climb such a chunk. El Capitan! Just the words brought a thrill to my young heart. As I got older and my climbing improved, people told me about some of the climbs they'd heard about on the big rock. I read as much as I could find on the subject of big walls—preferably El Cap, and began to have dreams about climbing El Cap myself.

When I got into college at age 16, I had little time to climb, yet climbing remained a major mental drive. After a couple of years of college, it seemed clear that I wanted something else. I began driving a rig for a living—but climbing lured me on. From my earliest climbs, I used climbing as a discipline to investigate myself. What could I do? What were my limitations? What kind of character did I have? What kind of character could I forge?

Throughout the years I made many trips to the valley, but lack of time kept me from doing what I wanted: to climb El Cap. It seemed to be a force calling me. I knew that harder climbs existed in other parts of the world, but El Cap had a special attraction.

Then I spent a week in the valley. I'd just read about some new climbs that were being touted as the hardest technical rock climbs in the world. I talked to the local climbers to find out what I could. It seemed that a few people were really pushing the wall-climbing standards.

Gazing upward, I made my usual stand in El Cap Meadow. The rock hadn't changed, of course, only the climbs on it were changing. The newer routes were getting much harder, more dangerous, more committing. And the same climbers' names kept appearing in all the climbing periodicals. I began to comprehend a little of the small handful of climbers who were pushing the standards. They were a breed set apart—the supermen.

I scanned all of El Cap. Where would they put a route up next? They seemed to chose blanker and blanker lines all the time. Peering through a pair of binoculars, I noticed a huge blank slab located in between "Aquarian Wall" and "Dihedral Wall." When would they get to it?

A couple of years later, that particular route still hadn't been taken. Harder and harder routes kept cropping up, but nobody seemed to want the slab. I wondered why. To me it seemed like the ultimate test of pure rock-climbing technique and equipment. In addition, I wondered what it would take in terms of human spirit. I had heard about 50-foot falls and longer. Looking back, I can't say exactly what attraction that slab had on me. It was just sweeping, shining blankness!

In 1980 I met Mark Smith. I used to joke with him that his name sounded like a good alias. Shortly after we began climbing together, Mark's mother died of cancer. Mark was stricken. He quit college, where he was in his third year of a computer science engineering course. A significant inheritance gave Mark a little breathing room to collect himself.

At this same time, I was fired from my well-paying trucking job. Because I had the most seniority, a new manager in the company decided to use me as an example of his power. I sued the company and won a sizable award.

Both Mark and I were totally burned out and at the point of transition. We began climbing together exclusively. We enjoyed each other's company and began a full-time endeavor climbing an obscure cliff called the Riverside Quarry. We spent six months living in San Bernardino, California, and climbing at the quarry. We put up 22 first ascents on the cliff. Each involved aid climbing on an overhanging, loose, 200-foot-high wall. We were terrified most of that six-month period. We produced a guidebook to the place— somehow broke even on our expenses and made a little money.

When we first moved in together, we made a trip to Yosemite. While we were there, I pointed out the slab on El Capitan. I casually mentioned to Mark that for years I had entertained fantasies of climbing it. Nobody else had been successful in putting a route up it yet, although some attempts had finally been made. Mark basically passed off my small talk. He had decided that there was no way he was interested in that slab—he wanted a long and full life!

◆ ◆ ◆

Once I realized my true relationship to Jesus, I saw myself as I really was. Next I began to have some comprehension of the life of victory He plans for me. I quickly saw that the Christian life would involve change and sacrifice. I could have looked for another standard of a "good life," but I knew that Jesus' life was the highest standard I could ever find.

For years I dreamed of that slab as the standard of pure rock wall climbing. It was a lofty enough goal to be intriguing; it was an elevated enough aspiration to move and motivate me. Likewise, if I shoot only for a second-rate standard of life, that's all I will ever attain. My goal must intrigue me enough to motivate me to struggle to attain it. The Bible standard is summed up in these two verses: "Therefore you are to be perfect, as your heavenly Father is perfect" (Matt. 5:48). "I press on toward the goal for the prize of the upward call of God in Christ Jesus" (Phil. 3:14).

Why does Paul press on toward that goal of perfection in Christ? For the prize that goes along with that upward call, "Come up higher!" Is it not the most intriguing and exalted aspiration to come up higher, higher, all the way to the standard of Christ's character?

Time passed as we climbed at the Quarry, and Mark began to get dragged into my scheme. Finally he committed to do the slab on El Capitan with me, though inwardly he wondered if it were possible. We had heard of failed attempts on the slab by other, well-known teams. We felt up to the technical end of it—the actual climbing. Our main worry was if we could cope with the day-in-and-day-out pressure of the climb. Especially the hauling of our bags concerned us. Would the problems of moving so much weight up the wall bog us down? We knew that the route would involve a lot of time: micro-flake sky hooking, hard free climbing, and obviously some amount of drilling.

The climb began in earnest months before we arrived in the valley. We purchased equipment, but many things were too expensive to buy so we made what we could. We bought bolts and hangers in bulk to cut costs. We bought rivets by the box. We made our own copperheads and portaledges.

After months of climbing, planning, and preparation, we left for the valley. We began our attempt on Wings of Steel (the name of our climb) early in the morning of May 4, 1982.

After years of pondering and restless waiting, the day of reckoning had arrived. Our most immediate concern was the huge pile of gear stashed in our tents. Could we move it all up the wall? Our calculations suggested we would have to live on the wall for a month. Were we deluded to think we could spend a month up there?

Instead of looking at the whole mound of gear in one mass, we had to look at it as the seven haul bags it would be, to be hauled up one by one, a little at a time. We could not yet grasp the thought of a month on the wall, but as we looked at the massive mound of gear, we thought that we had covered all contingencies. We gained more confidence in our six months of planning.

We hiked to the base of the slab and wandered back and forth, looking for the most likely line of weaknesses with which to start the climb. Just looking up at the slab and thinking about the audacity of our undertaking was enough to send chills through me.

After a few hours we agreed on the spot where Wings of Steel would leave the ground, and we determined that the next day we would begin work on the first two pitches. We hiked back to camp and began to rack up, all the while awash in waves of doubt and fear. As we racked, we talked. We gained courage from each other and cemented our resolve. We spent hours discussing a retreat, and decided that we were committed to the climb. Once we left the ground, we would rim out unless we were injured or the climbing became invalid in our minds. We made a vow to each other that neither of us would mention the "Q" word: QUIT! Our theory was that if neither of us started a discussion about quitting, we could never agree to quit.

We turned in that night with high hopes and soaring enthusiasm. That night I dreamed a vague dream about being "up there."

On May 5 we took care of some business in the valley and then headed for the wall. Our plan was to fix two pitches, move all the gear to the base, and then go for it in one push with no siege tactics. We wanted to fix two pitches because it seemed ridiculous to set up camp within one rappel of the ground. But the big reason to fix two pitches was to find out about the consistency of the hooking higher up and to see if it looked as though it would continue to be viable.

We got to the proposed start of our route, which had a scalloped-out section I hoped to free climb. We wanted to free climb anything that looked even remotely within our abilities. I was unsuccessful in making any real headway, so it would have to go on aid.

I placed the first copperhead of the climb, a #0. As I placed it, I was amazed that the little seam didn't crumble. The type of rock we were used to would not have held that head. El Cap rock is incredibly solid. Even so, I knew that the head wouldn't hold body weight, but I was right on the ground—so, I stood on it. Somehow it did hold—and Wings of Steel was under way!

Copperheads and hooks got me higher and higher off the ground. Far below me, a bolt had provided some security for a short time, but I was soon looking at a long ground fall. (We were willing to take long falls on the route, and had trained ourselves not to wilt at the prospect of one, but we were hoping to avoid grounding out.) When Mark started answering my questions diplomatically, I knew it was time for a bolt.

"Mark, am I going to ground out?"

"No, not yet."

A few more hook moves. Then, "Mark, how does it look?"

"Well, if the last rivet holds, . . . It still looks OK."

One more hook. "Mark, how about now?"

"Well, Rich, I'll do what I can for you. Ha, ha, ha!"

Mark thought my plight was serious, although he tried to maintain a comical demeanor. After placing the bolt, I felt much better. I knew that my risk of a ground fall on the pitch and, therefore, on the entire climb was now over. The thing you fear the most in any fall is hitting something, and the biggest thing you can hit is Mother Earth. I felt that now that prospect was behind me.

Numerous hooks and two more rivets brought me to a decision. I was three hooks out from the last rivet when I came to a very steep section. Suddenly all the flakes seemed to vanish. To my left the rock was slightly lower angled, and it appeared to be more featured in that direction as well. But there were no visible flakes, only slight depressions in the wall which we call "friction pockets."

Straight up I saw a few flakes, but they appeared sloped and loose. If I went up, I might get into an area of fewer flakes and, therefore, more drilling. I was already putting in drilled placements at a pretty good rate, but the climbing still seemed valid to me. But if I went up instead of left, maybe I would have to drill more. Bad route-finding could require so much drilling as to cost us the slab. We had to be very sensitive to where the tiny features of the slab were leading.

I looked again to my left and saw a small edge on the wall at foot level, but it was several feet away. Then I found some edges for my hands. They faced left and were tiny. They wouldn't hold hooks because they were sloped, but maybe my fingers could use them.

I looked up again and after confronting the blankness that loomed above, decided to try to free climb left. Evening shadows engulfed the valley, and I couldn't see how the hook I was on was still holding, so I decided to get out of there for the night. Looking at the rivet 10 feet below, I started to put in a bolt to protect the free climbing and then to lower myself to the ground.

I lowered from the bolt and looked up: a whole day for only 70 feet? Well, we could see we were right to plan for 30 days on the wall. Climbing the slab was going to be a slow process.

As we walked down the trail, we got into a deep discussion.

"It's not looking too good up there. If it doesn't go free out left, I don't know—I'll have to try to go up, and that looks pretty bad."

"Is it going to be viable to do this, Rich? I mean, we've already got about as high a drilling ratio as I'm happy with. What if the flakes aren't up there?"

"Then we're going to have to quit, because if this happens on the first pitch, it will happen all the way up the slab," I replied. "We've got to try this, and we're gonna give it our best shot before we quit. Somebody someday is going to do that slab. Why shouldn't it be us?"

"I hope the pitch works tomorrow. I wish I knew the route would go, but we probably won't know for sure all the way up," Mark observed. (Mark had his intuitions.)

Approaching the car, we lapsed into silence. We piled inside, and I pushed a favorite tape into the cassette player. Music has always inspired and encouraged me. As we listened to the tape on the way back to camp, I began to feel better. I felt very grateful for Mark.

We arrived back at camp and lowered our food from the bear cable. Dinner was no great experience, but for me a good meal doesn't have to consist of much. As they say, "It's the thought that counts."

At least my bed was comfortable. With four Ensolite pads under each of us, what more could we ask for?

The next morning we ate breakfast and went to the bank, where we found that it was Mark's birthday. Mark chortled that in the intensity of the climb, he had forgotten. We then returned to the wall.

I self-pulleyed my way back to the high bolt, this time with free-climbing shoes on. Looking left, I was somewhat dismayed. In the morning light the "holds" were not visible. But it still looked better than straight up.

Standing in a friction pocket near the bolt, I frantically started chalking little holds as far as I could reach. Then I found that little edge for my foot again. Keeping my eye on it, so as not to lose it,

I began to stem[1] over to it. Finally, at about the limit of my stemming ability, my toe made contact.

Moving my hands farther left, I chalked more holds for quick visibility. Then I began to pull onto the edge, out of the friction pocket. Just when I thought I was making it, I simultaneously found a good foot edge farther out left, but my left foot slipped off the edge it was on.

After pulleying myself back to the bolt and Mark giving happy chuckles, I tried again. I got my hand sequence crossed up and came off again. This time, I left some of my knuckle skin up there. At that point I was bleeding and beginning to feel frustrated. I tried again and this time was successful in pulling over on top of the left foot edge. A quick foot switch, fraught with desperation, and I was able to get my left foot on the somewhat decent edge farther out. I was now far enough from the bolt to be unwilling to lose those moves in a fall. I doubted I could repeat them again.

I couldn't stop where I was to place a bolt, and I couldn't find a hookable edge, so I moved on. After a couple of more upward and left moves, I located a hook edge. Clinging desperately, I clawed through the rack to find a Leeper narrow hook.[2] I placed it on the edge and transferred my weight onto the aiders.

I was in terror of the hook blowing, me falling, and being forced to try to repeat those moves again! But it didn't blow, and the bolt went in. By now Mark was cheering his approval.

The edges continued, and although they were sloped and not hookable, I was able to free climb. Fifteen feet later, I got in another bolt. And almost 20 feet after that another.

I hung on that last bolt, resting, and looked up. I was only about 50 feet below the bulge where we wanted to set up the anchor. But

---

[1] A "fun" maneuver that requires you to spread your legs farther and farther apart like the splits as your feet reach out for holds.

---

[2] This is the small 1/16-inch tipped hook referred to in the first chapter. It is good for about 200 pounds.

I could see that I wasn't going to be free climbing those last 50 feet. The wall got very steep again and was sprinkled with only the tiniest of flakes.

I could see I was in for more hooking, but I had high spirits because I could see that the pitch would get done, that it wouldn't take too many drilled placements, and that with only one more protection bolt, I should reach the belay bulge that day.

I enthusiastically top-looped the bolt and scanned the face for the best edge. I placed a hook on a likely candidate and transferred weight onto it. I was feeling good as it held.

As I approached my top-loops, our first major setback occurred. With my left foot in the second loop and my right in the top, I was just starting to stand up, when the hook creaked once—and the hook flake peeled off.

Just as the hook pinged, I pictured the four-inch-wide ledge from which I had placed the last bolt. I impacted it with my left foot just as the rope came tight. As I swung under the bolt, pain shot through my ankle.

Mark instantly sensed something was wrong. He shouted up to ask if I was all right. I just dangled and moaned quietly until the pain subsided to a bearable level.

"Rich, you OK?"

"Well, I don't think it's broken, but . . ." I tried to move it. "It's the worst sprain I've ever had. Mark, I just don't believe this!"

"Can you get yourself down?"

I was out over half the rope so I couldn't be lowered to the ground on the lead rope.

"Yeah, lower me to the next bolt."

As Mark complied, I got out a pair of aiders. When I got to the bolt, Mark stopped lowering, and I leaned over and clipped into the bolt. As I stood on the bolt in aiders, Mark fed enough slack into the lead rope for me to tie some knots. I tied the bolt I was on in with the uppermost bolt, to make a two bolt anchor. The anchor thus secure, I tied in the haul line. Mark took me off belay, and I rappelled the haul line to the ground.

Once on the ground, I tried to hobble over to Mark, but my left ankle would not support any weight. So I hopped over on one foot and sat down on a rock. I couldn't figure it out. It didn't hurt very much anymore. A sprain should be hurting more as it swelled. But there was no swelling. Not much pain and no swelling, yet it wouldn't support weight. I didn't think it was broken, so I couldn't figure it out. One thing was sure, though, I wasn't going to be climbing for a while. After a silence, we began to discuss our options.

"OK, I can't climb, but we're only 50 feet from the belay. What about you going up and finishing the pitch?"

"Yeah . . ." Mark was unimpressed. "I guess I could do that, but what about getting you down the trail? It's going to be dark in a few hours."

"We've got our headlamps, and you can get me a staff to use."

"OK, I'll go up and give it a shot."

"Well . . . wait, Mark! We could just hobble out of here right now and wait until my ankle heals. Then I'll lead the top of it."

"No. We can get this pitch up today. We don't know what's wrong with your ankle. It could heal in a couple of days, or it could take a couple of months. If there is any substantial ligament damage—who knows? At least if the pitch is up and cleaned, we can bail the route if you don't heal in some reasonable time."

Mark knew about ligament damage. The ligaments in his right knee were shot as a result of a football incident. The doctors had said that surgery was his only option for a full recovery. "Ligaments don't really heal," Mark said, "but we will feel better if the pitch is up."

"OK. I can belay just fine."

I knew that Mark wasn't too happy about having to lead on this pitch. He certainly hadn't expected to have to lead one of my pitches at all, and it was all hooking up there. But, he figured, it was his birthday, what could happen?

Somewhat unenthusiastically, Mark jumarred up to my anchor. I put him on belay as he untied the knots and tied into the lead rope. He then self-pulleyed himself up to the top bolt. Surveying the situation, he decided to go right and up, instead of left as I had.

Then he planned to cross back left, after the danger of impacting the little ledge had passed.

Mark found an edge and hooked it. He moved into his aiders, covering the hook with his hand. This would keep the hook from planting itself in his face if it pinged off while he was low in his aiders. He moved up in his aiders, until he was in the top-loops.

I was holding my breath. Top-looping is very hard on hooks. Being in the top-loops puts an outward leverage on the hook. In addition, if one's weight is not centered exactly below the hook, the hook will shift to the side and ping off.

The hook kept holding while Mark found another edge. He hooked it and moved up, taking the first hook off its flake to be reused higher up. Then another hook. And another.

The tension built as he got farther from the bolt: the risk multiplied as the potential fall lengthened and as the amount of time to be lost in a fall increased. Finally, about 25 feet out from the bolt, Mark stopped. Top-looping a hook, he had decided to put in a bolt. He said that he would go from the bolt he was placing to the belay bulge, only 25 feet above him.

Top-looping a bad hook to place a bolt is almost unbearable. It takes a half hour to place a bolt, and during that time you don't dare shift your weight one iota. Your feet go to sleep, then your calves. Your feet hurt intensely from the aiders digging into them, but you can't shift your weight. Any weight change can cause the hook to shift and—flight time. But finally Mark got the bolt in and stood on it.

After resting a couple of minutes to get feeling in his toes again, Mark top-looped the bolt. Finding another hook placement, he moved higher.

Four hooks higher, Mark reached the bulge. Two more placements and he could put in the belay bolts. Standing on his best hook so far, he searched for another placement.

Fortunately, he found a very thin short copperhead seam to his left. Unfortunately, it was facing away from him and almost out of reach. This presented a problem. He wouldn't be able to see the head as he mashed it into place with his left hand. Mark is not left-handed. He wondered about just using another hook, but then he considered his position. He was more than 20 feet out from the last bolt with nothing in between him and it. A fall from his position was certain to be at least 40 feet long. The hook he was on was a Leeper broad on an excellent flake. A sense of security permeated the placement. To move off of it would put him back in the realm of insecurity. The problem: how to find the two most secure placements past the bulge.

It had taken more than two hours to cover the last 20 feet. He didn't want to lose the ground gained with a less than one-second fall. The copperhead, if it was good, might hold a fall from at least the next placement above. So if the hook above the head blew out, the head might hold, and the full 40- to 50-foot fall might be avoided.

Mark began to place the copperhead, a #0. He had to lean as far to the left as he could without falling out of his aiders. He would tap on the head with his left hand. Then he would holster his hammer and feel the placement with his left hand. Then grab the hammer and tap some more.

Finally he had it in as well as he could get it by feel. Ten minutes spent on the head; the moment of truth had arrived. He clipped aiders into the head and began to weight it with his left foot, keeping his right foot in the hook aiders.

I was impressed! It took an effort of will to move onto that head, a blind placement, while facing such a fall.

As he moved over farther and farther, he was forced to get unbalanced on the hook, which made it more and more impossible to get back upright on the hook if the head failed. Then came the moment when he could lean just a little more and get his first look at the placement.

Just as he looked, and with one foot still in the hook aiders, the copperhead pulled out. Mark made a heroic attempt to get back to the hook, but he was too far to the left. The aider on his right foot caught and turned him upside down, with his back facing the wall. Then the hook went "ping!"

Upside down, Mark hurtled down the slab! I pulled in some

rope through my belay plate, then locked it off. Mark went into a scooped out section of the rock and was tossed away from the wall. Just as he contacted rock again, the rope went tight, and he slid horizontally across the wall for 12 feet until he was under the bolt!

It was awesome—the most spectacular fall I had ever seen! Before I could even open my mouth, Mark said, "Believe it or not, I'm OK!" Then he pulled himself upright to survey his damages. His head had come within one foot of the ledge that had cost me my ankle! The five feet of rope I had pulled in at the start of Mark's fall had shortened his fall and saved his life.

Aside from a lacerated elbow and some harness bruises on his hips, he was OK—physically. Mentally? Only time would tell how much of a setback the fall had been.

It was evening, so he did not have enough time to go back up. Besides, he had had enough flight time for the day, so I lowered him down to the next bolt. He set up an anchor and rappelled the haul line as I had done.

We felt very battered and beaten at that moment. We sat for a minute, then Mark went into the woods to find me a staff while I thought about his 45-foot fall. The climbing was desperately hard! How badly was I hurt? How long before we could try again? Did we really want to try again?

Stumbling out the mile of talus and trail took several hours. My ankle didn't hurt unless I tried to put weight on it, and then the pain was searing. I broke the staff about half way down the trail and had to fall down to keep the weight off my ankle. Mark found a new staff, and we moved on by headlamp.

We reached the car in pitch blackness, and Mark drove us back to camp. Without eating we crawled into bed at 11:00 p.m. A great birthday for Mark.

Our first attempt on our climb ended with us being the obvious losers. While we still had a rope fixed to our high point, we were lost in deep discouragement. The climbing was much harder and more dangerous than we had anticipated. It would require more trauma and effort from us than we had planned to endure. We had to assess our goal and decide if it was worth the pain. I, for one, was in some real pain. And Mark was suffering serious doubts about the value of the project in the face of the risks.

"Nothing of value is free. Even the breath of life is purchased at birth only through gasping effort and pain" (Robert A. Heinlein, *Starship Troopers*).

Once I confront the standard of Christ's character, and determine to become like Him, I still must count the cost. While the goal seems interesting, even intriguing, I am not able to foresee the efforts and pains I will suffer to obtain it. Only as I endure struggles with myself and others can I honestly appraise the value of the goal I have set. Will it remain my dream? Will I keep my determination? Only time can tell as, even now, I continue to weigh the pain against the rewards.

◆ ◆ ◆

The morning of May 7 arrived in a drizzle. I woke up and for a while listened to the rain on the dome. Mark had been awake for some time already.

I tried to move my ankle: no go. The pain was quite bad unless I left it alone. I decided to stay in the dome until the rain stopped or my ankle got better or the urge to go to the bathroom became too strong or any combination thereof.

Mark went out into the rain to lower the food from the bear cable. He searched through the food bag until he found something we could eat that didn't have to be cooked. We were wet, cold, discouraged, and in pain. At this point we weren't even sure it was feasible to continue the climb. We both had the same thought: Maybe we should just go back up to the wall and pull our ropes down—simply concede that we were in over our heads and admit defeat.

———— ♦ ————

CHAPTER 4

Hooks, Hooks, and Yet More Hooks

Mark clambered back into the dome, wet and uncomfortable. We ate; time passed. I read; Mark moped. Mark read; I moped. Finally I had to make the inevitable 100-yard journey to the bathroom.

Standing up and grasping my staff, I surveyed the terrain. Sunnyside Campground was nothing more than a dripping swamp! Five other campsites were completely submerged in water. We had unwittingly pitched the dome in what had become a small lake.

I planted the staff forward and to my left. Then I hopped, on my right foot, up to meet it. I selected another solid spot for the staff and hopped forward to join it. Every hop created splashes of muddy water, which coated my lower legs.

After about five minutes of effort, the journey reached its end. The terror of a miss hop, and its resulting mud-wallow, passed for a time.

Cold, wet, and in pain, all too soon I again stood in the doorway of the bathroom and tried to gather the resources for the return journey. Staring at the dismal landscape, I wondered what we were doing in the valley during (statistical fact) the worst post-winter runoff year of the century. The possibility of succeeding on our route seemed very remote.

With no major mishaps, I arrived back at the dome. I squatted down to climb in, and my ankle gave an audible crack. The pain was the worst I have ever felt! I grew nauseated as I tumbled inside.

The pain stopped as my ankle stopped bearing weight, and the nausea quickly passed.

I thought it was all over. I figured that I had cracked a bone in the fall and had just broken it completely! I then tried to move the foot, and to my surprise, was quite successful. Since there was no crackling inside, I once again came to my original conclusion: no break—a very frustrating mystery. The thought of a dislocation never occurred to me until long after the climb was over.

I changed clothes and put an elastic bandage on my injured foot then settled into my sleeping bag for the rest of the afternoon.

It rained through the Sabbath, and through May 9. We spent our time reading, sleeping, eating, talking, and making occasional forays to the bathroom. We thought about our ropes hanging part way up the first pitch of our new route.

My ankle felt better after the big crackle and began to improve. By May 10, I could hobble about without the staff. That afternoon the weather began to clear up. The rain stopped, and the temperature went up a few degrees. I could now put a fair amount of weight on my ankle (with some pain), but nevertheless, it would hold weight and I could "walk." We decided that if the weather stayed clear and my ankle felt up to it, we would go back to work on the first pitch the next day. Mark would lead, of course.

Tuesday, May 11, dawned bright and clear. We awoke, ate, and began to rack gear. My ankle felt better once the morning stiffness left it. Howard came by our campsite. Mark knew him from Los Angeles. He wanted to accompany us to the base of the wall and see what was going on. I was glad for his company; he could help carry gear up the talus.

We drove to the base, divided loads, and started up the trail. Several times on the way up I stepped on a rock, and it shifted or turned under my ankle. Each time I had to stop until the pain subsided. Even wearing an elastic bandage and stepping cautiously, I found walking on talus an insecure experience! I had to decide if I was going to weight one ankle and hop, or weight both ankles and walk. Since one can't hop up a talus slope, I opted to walk.

When we arrived at the base, Mark was pretty terrified to go up and give a repeat performance of his flight! Howard was concerned that Mark might not. He joked with Mark that he had hiked all that way, and he didn't intend to hike down disappointed. Mark said that he would see what he could do and began his jumar up the ropes to the high point.

Reaching the high bolt, Mark got up into his top-loops. He had one thing in his favor: Since the hooks he would be using had held his weight before, they should do it again.

The first hook had Mark in total horror. The mind plays games—tries to think up a ploy—a way to avoid what seems inevitable. Yet after a long pause to pray and gather courage, Mark hooked the first minuscule flake again. It held. Top-looping that one, he hooked the next flake, then the next one, then the next. His horror faded as he progressed, only to be replaced with a pervasive low-level anxiety. The problem: locating his previous hook placements to use them again. Which flakes had held his weight? And which were just untested potential falls?

After hours of intense concentration and fear, Mark hooked onto the bulge where we had planned to set up the first anchor. The first 1/4-inch bolt went in very quickly since his fatigue in placing it was offset by his desire to get off the hook and onto the bolt. After planting the bolt and hastily clipping aiders into it, he tromped right up into the aiders, clipped his waist loop in, and began to breathe massive sighs of relief! The threat of the long fall was over for the first pitch.

The 3/8-inch bolt took a couple of hours to place. Mark complained that we really didn't need it, but I was adamant. Every belay would have one 3/8-inch bolt in it. We would have an awesome amount of weight hanging on those anchors. We had estimated that approximately 1,400 pounds would hang from the second belay anchor, which would also act as our first bivy anchor.

Mark didn't complain much, and when it was almost dark, the anchor was in. Mark anchored the ropes and rappelled off. By the light from our headlamps, we carefully hiked down to camp.

May 12 we checked the mail again then headed up the trail. Again my ankle twisted a few times. The pain was enough to make me think about tabling the climb until I completely healed. But we didn't want to be on the wall during the hottest months of the year.

Mark cleaned the pitch and racked his gear while I got into my hammock to belay in comfort. A belay seat just doesn't make it for a long belay. A hammock offers full body support and the ability to adjust into different positions. By the time I was in the hammock, I hung about six feet below the belay bolts.

Finished racking, Mark tied in and gave me a long look as I put his lead rope through my belay plate. In that look I saw how much Mark wanted the climb. I saw the fear—he didn't delude himself about the risks. I saw him weighing the risks against the climb and really wondering how they stacked up. The risks were real. The route might not be.

Mark top-looped the bolt farthest to the left and ran the rope through a carabiner at the belay. The hook edges were there. The climb could go on. He hooked an edge then top-looped. Then another hook, top-loops again. Then a third hook, all Leeper narrows. Mark got into the second loops on the third hook when it pinged!

Mark shot past me. The rope came tight and launched me right up into the belay bolts. What an impact! Fortunately, the fall was clean, and Mark was unhurt. He hauled himself back to the belay and lowered me the six feet back down into my hammock. The fall was about 25 feet, a great way to start the day's climbing!

With another long look, Mark got back onto the bolt. The first two hooks held again, and Mark found another flake for the third hook. He hooked it and got clear up to his top-loops. Suddenly, Mark looked down at me—and the hook made the dreaded *ping*.

Mark flew passed me again. I was launched into the bolts yet again! Again he was unhurt—physically. Mark got back up to the anchor bolt and asked me flatly if we were crazy. Sure, there were hook flakes. The route could go, but at this percentage of hook failure we would be raw meat before the climb was finished! During the first 150 feet of the climb, we had taken a combined total of 120 feet in falls. The slab was 1,200 feet high. If this ratio continued, . . . Mark didn't want to take his share of the 1,000 feet in falls.

I understood his problem. The leading was a horror. But I had found a new problem: We had hoped to be able to relax while belaying, a kind of reprieve from the leading, yet I was finding the belaying to be pretty bad. I was learning to hate the ping that a hook makes when all the tension in the metal is suddenly and irrevocably released—then the awesome impact.

Maybe I'd have to become less empathetic in order to survive belaying. Looking grim, Mark top-looped the belay bolt, then moved onto the first hook, then the second. He top-looped it and searched the face. Nothing! He had used up the two flakes within his reach. He scrounged around awhile and then pulled out the drill.

The first rivet took about 15 minutes to place. Mark happily rested a moment on it, yet (too soon for him) he realized that he had to move on. Two more hooks brought him to another blank spot. In went another rivet.

At this point Mark was able to go about 25 feet on hooks. Each successive hook increased his chance of pulling the rivets below him and adding 20 to 40 feet to whatever distance he would fall. Those 25 feet took hours of concentration, precise judgment, and untold mental anguish.

Finally, he could take the strain no longer, and he stopped to plant a bolt—50 feet above the first belay—a potential fall of between 80 and 100 feet!

Yet another evening descended upon us, so I lowered Mark back to the first belay. He was elated by how well the second pitch was shaping up. And he had good reason to congratulate himself!

Although terrified by the day's climbing, Mark could see a good-looking copperhead seam, which should be easier climbing. Also he was developing an ability to push the potential fall into the back of his mind.

We hiked down, drove back to camp, ate, and went to bed. Before going to sleep, we decided to rate the day's climbing A5. That night I dreamed about falling and falling, and then the pain in my ankle returned.

◆ ◆ ◆

Mark had decided, even if unknown to him at the time, that the goal was worth the risk. He had crossed a fine line into the realm where, whatever the risk, whatever the pain, whatever the sacrifice, he would try his best to move toward the goal. He had counted the cost and had achieved a resigned outlook about the climb.

When I first encounter real difficulty in my Christian life, I am confronted with some choices. Will I go all the way with Jesus, no matter what the sacrifice? Or will I begin to live a formal, social religion that is devoid of real power because it no longer addresses the deep flaws of character that every Christian must confront and overcome to remain a Christian?

If I no longer confront wrong habits and traits of character and cherished sins that keep me from attaining the goal, I am no longer really on the climb. The climb appears too painful, too dangerous, too much of a sacrifice. From that time on, although I may talk of the Christian life, I do not live it. If I would remain a Christian, I must climb! I cannot honestly call myself a climber when I am retreating from the climb.

◆ ◆ ◆

The next morning was clear, but cold. On the hike up, my ankle gave out twice. Each time I felt pain and frustration well up in me. Would I be able to lead at all? We would have the first two pitches fixed soon. The third lead was mine. I figured that in less than a week I would have to lead. I couldn't expect Mark to lead everything. Although we were making headway on the climb, I wasn't healing very quickly.

We jumarred our fixed ropes to the first belay, where I settled into my hammock to belay in comfort again. Mark racked up, a quick task, and self-pulleyed himself up to his high point. Once he had secured himself at that bolt, he looked around to determine the best way to get over to the copperhead seam. It was obviously going to take some more frightening hooking. When Mark looked down my way, he didn't appear to be too happy. I could hear him muttering to himself under his breath.

Mark's mental gymnastics were crystal clear. First, elation at how well the pitch was going. This feeling usually occurs at the end of a day of leading, when the terror has dissipated. Second, the terror returns, as a new day of leading begins. Third, the terror is coupled with helplessness. How to avoid it? How to get out of it? Fourth, a grim determination begins to pervade the consciousness. The determination becomes coupled with a motivation to do a good job.

At the start of each day of leading, Mark had to go through this scenario, and each time he had to decide if it was worth it. Each time he had to convince himself that it was. He would look down at me as if to say "This is your idea, you dragged me into this, and convinced me it was worthwhile. Now I'm strung out, and you're hurt! Is it still a good idea? Why don't we leave this for another time, or another climbing team?"

As I remembered my responsibility in coercing him into the present fiasco, Mark top-looped the bolt and quickly found an edge. He put a Leeper narrow on it and transferred his weight. It held. He was right at the bolt, so it involved little fear factor. He top-looped that hook and got another, then another—all Leeper narrows.

Yet another day turned into evening. Yet again we rappelled, leaving ropes fixed to our high point and retreating to the known comforts of the ground.

Mark woke me up the next morning. May 14 had arrived in a cloud cover. The day's leading did not appeal to him, especially when viewed in comparison to just spending the chilly day in bed. But were we not men? We wondered.

Finally, we did muster up the fortitude to get out of bed. We then commenced the typical morning scenario. Lower the food bag from the bear cable. Rummage through the contents. Make the important decision—will we cook or eat cold? Stare dismally at the assortment of possibilities. Raisin bran again? Drag the spoils onto the table. Wipe the dew off of everything. Sit down to the realization that we didn't get all the moisture off the bench. Mix powdered milk, and munch out. We invariably chose to eat cold food for breakfast. We reserved the time and luxury of cooking for dinner.

While eating we had one top priority: find a ray of sun between the pine trees and absorb a little warmth. That morning we were unable to find any sunlight of enough intensity to cut through the envelope of cold air.

After parking the car at El Cap meadow we started the hike to the base. We arrived at the base of the route with only one turn to my ankle. It was getting stronger.

Mark got to the high bolt, clipped aiders in, and moved up onto them. It had become a familiar pattern. He would pause to gather his nerve, then top-loop the bolt and find a hook placement. Then slowly he would transfer weight over to the hook aiders. The hook would creak but hold, and he would move up onto it.

Mark moved from one hook to another until (about three hooks above the bolt) he was able to get his fingers into a large copperhead seam. Mark buried a #2 head that seemed really solid and stood on it. Top-looping, he pegged in another #2 head, which was also very good. Then it started to rain.

Mark stood on his highest copperhead and started to mash another. This time a #0. It rained harder. Mark got onto the #0 head and moved up in his aiders. It poured.

I tied Mark off and sent his rain gear up on the haul line. Then I got into my poncho and attempted to get into a position where rain landed on the smallest amount of exposed surface area.

By this time we could see how the seams were formed. Water poured down the copperhead seam and channeled down the rope—into my belay plate and onto my lap. I tried to remain impassive about what was becoming a miserable day.

By the afternoon, I was pretty cold and wet. Mark, who at least was able to keep somewhat warm through movement, was having trouble placing heads in the running water of the seam. I couldn't look up at Mark because my glasses got soaked; the raindrops on the lenses made me feel like I had insect eyes with compound lenses.

The rain, if it could be possible, got more intense. My poncho was not intended for that kind of treatment—especially with me in belay position—and was only keeping a small percentage of the water out. Once we were living on the wall, we did not intend to climb through the rain. The portaledges would be nearby, and their rain flies were designed to keep us cozy in just such circumstances. Also, climbing in the rain is a much more delicate and dangerous proposition. Slippery rock is much more unforgiving of a slight loss of balance. Wet ropes do not hold falls as well as dry ones. The impact force is greatly increased, so the tendency to zip placements out of the wall is correspondingly increased. These added dangers were the primary reason not to climb in the rain. However, Mark had to get in some decent placements from which to lower off.

After more hooking, Mark came to a blank spot. He stood in the rain and felt the wet rock. Nothing. He top-looped carefully. On the slick rock, it wouldn't be hard to have his feet slide over and cause his hook to shift and come off.

He felt the rock for a nubbin or edge. Nothing as far as he could reach. He pulled out the drill for a rivet. As he drilled, we discussed going down for the day. Progress was slow and dangerous in the rain, and we both felt uncomfortable. After I lowered Mark from the rivet, we rappelled to the ground.

The rain tapered off a little as we stashed our gear in the woods. By the time we reached camp, the sky cleared. Yet it remained very cold.

Howard came by camp that evening, and we went to the lodge to play some Scrabble. It was good to forget about the horror for a while. We went to bed, looking forward to the Sabbath: a whole day of not having to think about or work on our climb.

We passed the Sabbath with short hikes to pretty spots in the valley, reading, and dozing in the sun.

CHAPTER 5

The Slog!

S unday, the 16th, dawned bright and clear. We felt enthusiastic as we got up and ate. After the usual routine of hiking to the base, jumarring, and leading, Mark got our second pitch up. He drilled four bolts for our bivy anchor, fixed the ropes down from the second belay, and rappelled to the first anchor where I was.

We fixed two more lines from the first belay to the ground, stacked ourselves with the excess gear not in use at the two anchors, and rappelled to the ground. The first two pitches were fixed! Those pitches were costly, not merely in terms of time.

The next day we began to sort gear to go up to the base. We planned on hiking loads to the start of the route by Wednesday or Thursday. Although we were happily in a new phase of the climb, we could see that the packing and sorting phase would take some time. But what a relief not to be on hooks for a while!

The 17th and 18th passed this way: We took care of business in the valley—mail, bank, last-minute purchases, etc. Then we returned to camp and divided the gear into piles that would fit into a haul bag. We had to see what we could get into each haul bag and still maintain organization. We knew that we couldn't search through the haul bags to find an item we wanted once we were up there.

We even packed our 200 liters of water bottles, empty, into haul bags to test the fit. In dismay we realized that all the bottles just wouldn't fit into the two bags we had planned for them. It appeared that we would have to take less water and even use part of the gear haul bag for some water bottles.

We saved the food packing for last. Wednesday, the 19th, we parked the car in the Deli parking lot in Yosemite Village, so that we could be near the store for any last-minute purchases. We pulled our two huge bags of food out of the car, turned on the stereo, and went to work.

The first order of the day was to sort our canned food into day rations. We intended to have every item of food placed into one or two day bundles—packaged in small plastic garbage bags. This way we could just reach into the haul bag and grab a bag full of food, one for each day.

First, we laid out 30 stacks each of entree foods. One entree for the morning, one for the evening. For example: a can of tuna for the morning meal, and a can of vegetarian fried-chicken for the evening meal.

To supplement the entree foods, we added cans of fruit and vegetables for each meal. We had planned meals to approximate our usual meals at home in terms of variety and calories: about 3,000 calories per day.

In addition, we took along all types of munchies. Pop Tarts, raisins, dates, rolled and dried fruits, candy of all types, Figurine bars, almonds, granola bars, and pudding headed the list. We distributed the munchies through each day's food bundle, with variety the prime directive. If one day's bundle was a little bland, we would add smoked almonds and pudding. If another day's bundle was pretty interesting, we might add only some raisins or granola bars. In this way, we saw to it that each bundle of the 30 days' food was consistently interesting and provided sufficient calories.

Since there would be no stove, hence no luxury of cooking on the wall, we had to use only foods that needed no cooking and could keep for a month. No point in bringing dehydrated foods, because we would just have to haul the extra water along to rehydrate them, and the actual net weight in our haul bags would be the same.

We measured powdered milk and Instant Breakfast mix into small plastic bags. By pouring the pre-measured mix into half a liter of water and shaking, we could add some variety to what we drank. It would be almost a shake!

We ripped open the packaging on the dates and raisins, and put them into plastic bags to be distributed around in the food bundles. I opted for one-day food bundles. Mark chose to put two days' worth of food in each of his bundles. In this way our food haul bags could not get mixed up.

Finally, we both had our food sorted, packaged, and bundled. Thirty bundles for me, 15 for Mark, each of them triple bagged for strength. We repacked the bundles into our haul bags, and hefted them into the back of my car.

The food packing was done. All that remained was to fill the water bottles and transfer the bulk from the valley floor to the top of the second pitch. We would begin the task of moving loads the next day.

We went to bed early. Howard had said that he would help us get the first loads up to the base the next day. We wanted to begin early in the morning and get the two food bags to the base. We intended to hang the bags from trees at the base until we could haul everything off the ground at one time. Then we would make up all our actual haul bags, get them off the ground, and go for it! We expected to be on the route for good by Monday or Tuesday of the coming week!

Thursday dawned bright—a good day. Howard came by as we finished eating. We did dishes, then got into the car and buzzed down to the wall at a speed that demonstrated our enthusiasm. We divided my 125-pound food bag into three loads, one load for each of us. We also included a rope and a canvas bag for use in hanging the food in a tree (animal proof) then started up the trail.

As we hiked, for some reason a pervasive feeling of impending doom permeated my thoughts. I tried to shake it, but couldn't. We hadn't seen the route for days. I forced the feeling away.

When we got within sight of the route, I couldn't see our ropes. *I must be at the wrong angle,* I thought. But as I approached, I suddenly felt weak. The ropes were down. The bolts were gone. I dropped my pack and sat down at the base of what had once been our route.

During the past several days, some local climbers (upset that we were doing the route) had ascended our ropes, chopped our bolts and rivets from the wall, and rappelled back to the ground, pulling down our fixed ropes. This effectively erased our route.

I stared up. The anchor bolts were still in place—with rappel slings. I felt rage well up in me as Mark and Howard approached. Then I noticed the smell.

I inspected the ropes on the ground. They were a tangled mess. Somebody had put some time into that. There was a can of chili rubbed through the pile with the can on top. But I could tell that the odor wasn't chili. I struggled to accept the fact that the ropes had human excrement rubbed through them. The chili was merely a disguise.

"Look what they did to the ropes! Who did this? Why would they have done it?" My mind was full of angry and confused thoughts. I was full of rage, but weak at the same time. I just couldn't understand it.

I walked back down the trail past Mark and Howard. I had to get away. "The route has been chopped! The ropes are on the ground with human waste all through them."

"Ahhh . . . Come on, Rich!"

"Go on up and see. It's gone. All that work is just—well—it's over!"

I had to leave. I no more than arrived at the car when I started back up the trail. Mark and Howard might need help getting the bag into a tree. The food bag was heavy. On the way up, I wondered why I even cared. Let them just bring the food back down. NO! I couldn't see letting these people think that they had won. Suddenly the climb became more than just a dream I had entertained for years. We had to climb our route; we had a point to make!

New tactics would have to be developed, new attitudes sustained. These people would have to be taken seriously. How to find out who had participated in the act? We couldn't guard the wall day and night.

How to get at the root of the problem and eliminate it in order to keep climbing? It was clear that the climb couldn't go on until the problem was solved or stifled. They could cut us down any time our backs were turned.

I arrived at the base to find Mark and Howard staring bleakly upward. The belay bolts were still up there—but so inaccessible! I began to feel a good clean fury. The kind of righteous indignation that gets things done.

"All right, let's get the bag up in a tree!"

"Why? They'll just cut it down."

"Listen, they're not going to snuff us out!"

"Well, it doesn't look too good."

"No, but we'll work it out. We'll find out who did this. They surely can't get any backing in the rest of the valley about this. No matter what happens, we can't quit! Not until it's just impossible to go on." I even began to believe my own speech.

"OK, so we get this up in a tree. Then what?"

"We get the rest of the gear up here and then put up the first two pitches again. We just start over."

Howard joined in then. "Well, they chopped off your rivets flush with the wall. The holes aren't usable. New holes will have to be drilled. That's a lot of work!"

"We don't have much choice," responded Mark.

"That's right, Mark. We can't let them think that they can do whatever they want to anybody who, in their opinion, steps on their toes."

"Yeah. There's a principle here now."

"Now you're talking, Mark! We're not done yet."

"All right, we'll string your food up, Rich, pick up our gear, and get it cleaned up. Are we going to put up the same two pitches? I know I don't want to repeat a good section of that. I've already taken my share of falls!"

"We'll talk about that later. First, let's get to the root of our problem. Namely, the twisted attitude of whoever did this."

We tossed a rope over a tree limb and pulled my food haul bag into the air, then tied off the rope and got the spare canvas bag out. We gingerly maneuvered the tangled ropes and gear into the bag and tied it shut, sealing in the stench. We tied the bag, with its unsavory contents inside, onto a pack and hiked out.

Back at camp we began to ask around. Howard had a friend in

Rescue Site. He would see what he could find out. He recommended that we talk to the rangers about our problems. We were loath to drag them into it. We felt that it would complicate more than it would solve—at least until we had some kind of proof—so we just confined ourselves to asking around. During the course of the next several days, the story unfolded.

The people at Rescue Site claimed responsibility for the chopping. Attempting to conceal their jealousy and territorial attitude, they labeled us the "Mad Bolters," derided us for "over drilling" the route, and accused us of "raping" the slab. Of course, they could do the route in much better style, so we had no right even to attempt the climb!

Attempts to talk with the local climbers were fruitless. They were determined that we would not do the route. They threatened violence and damage to my car if we attempted to proceed.

Contacting the rangers proved a mistake. Rescue Site seemed to have endless credibility, and suddenly it seemed that we were on trial. Although officials didn't agree with Rescue Site's response to our climb, they felt that ours was the greater transgression. For almost two weeks we were bounced from office to office as we told our story to different rangers with different titles. Sunnyside rangers, sympathetic to Rescue Site's cause, raised our camping rates on three separate occasions. Each time, refusing to be discriminated against, we took this up with the administrative rangers, who informed the Sunnyside rangers that congress mandates camping fees and that we must be charged the same as anyone else. Arguing with the rangers about petty matters like camping fees made us feel as though we won small battles while we slowly lost the war.

We prayed unendingly that God would take up our cause. We were convinced that we were right. More and more we had a sense that this climb was deeply important in some way. We believed that God was with us, yet we could only see more and more trouble ahead. We clung to our belief that God would see us through, and we looked for ways to continue making progress.

Finally, our latest camping fee dispute brought us into contact with John Daley, the head ranger during daylight hours. He had heard of our conflict and seemed overjoyed to talk with us.

For the first time we felt that someone was really listening! After hearing our story, John said that he would support our climb and that he would inform the necessary people (Rescue Site included) that we must be allowed to continue the climb. This he called the "official" decision.

The attitude in the valley grew sullen. What Rescue Site could not accomplish via ranger support, they attempted to accomplish via climber support. They started a smear campaign unprecedented in climbing history. The primary charge: We were drilling a bolt-ladder right up the side of El Cap. It seemed as if the entire valley believed that we were unprincipled punks who wanted only to destroy the sacred El Cap. Even visiting climbers from other countries took Rescue Site's side. Everywhere we went people pointed, stared, and cursed at us.

We simply couldn't believe it! We were only trying to climb our route. None of these people had even seen the route. They didn't even care to find out that Rescue Site was lying about our drilling. They just hopped onto the bandwagon. Graffiti even appeared on the bathroom walls, suggesting strange things that the "Mad Bolters" should attempt to do.

Since we were officially allowed to proceed, we determined to press forward. The threats of violence continued, but we decided to ignore them and to hope that they amounted to nothing. We decided to make tracks while we could!

◆ ◆ ◆

Ancient Proverb

When your boat is in the middle of a dark and stormy sea, pray for God's help—and row toward shore.

There have been many times when I have been cut down in my attempt to live a Christian life. Perhaps I have yielded to temptation or responded to a situation in an un-Christlike manner. When this happens disappointment, frustration, and hopeless anxiety result. I wonder if I am still on the climb. I wonder if I will ever be able to get up the route.

Once I have been cut down and feel beaten back, the answer to one question determines my fate: Am I committed to the climb? Such a simple question, yet the answer decides my future course. If the climb has been painful so far and only the prospect of more pain to come seems apparent, the temptation to quit is strong—as if it is just not worth it. But am I committed to the climb?

When I feel most ashamed of myself, Jesus wants to reassure me. He points me to His life and His perfect self-control, and He assures me that He will make this a reality in my life. He invites me to grasp His hand again, and He puts me back onto the climb.

I am amazed at the commitment He has toward me and my salvation. I read again what He did in Gethsemane. I want to be like that!

Jesus knows my weaknesses and wants to help me overcome my faults and difficulties. He allows circumstances to assail my faith so that I can see the faults of character I still possess, so that I will sense my need of Him and stay—repentant—at His feet. Then He moves into my repentant heart and empowers it, motivates it, puts the stamp of His own character upon it, and I can continue climbing.

Am I committed to that climb? If so, then I can expect and act upon the help that Jesus has promised. Understanding what cut me down helps me reach my high point once again, this time with a deeper sense of dependence on Him, which helps me climb higher.

◆ ◆ ◆

By May 27, thanks to John Daley, we were finally in a position to begin work on the climb again. But how to begin? We had spent much time trying to figure out how to get back up to our second pitch anchor, without having to redo our first two pitches. We had noticed a left-facing dihedral to the left of our first two pitches and knew that it had been done because there were rappel bolts at the top. We later found out that Tony Yaniro had worked on the slab using this dihedral.

Originally we had opted not to use this dihedral to start the slab because there were no dihedrals higher up. No point in getting up two pitches, by way of a dihedral system, only to discover the real story higher up! If the route couldn't be done in good style right from the ground—without the dihedral—it couldn't be done.

So we had done two pitches, in good style, to the right of the dihedral. They had been chopped. Now we considered the dihedral. It was going to be much quicker and easier than repeating our original two pitches. The only problem would be getting over to our highest anchor. Since we couldn't see drilling another anchor within 50 feet of the our original second anchor, we determined to gain height in the dihedral, work our way over to the right, then up into our original second pitch anchor bolts. There was still going to be a lot of hooking to do.

The mail revealed that it would be good for me to return to Los Angeles briefly to deal with some paperwork from my trucking lawsuit. Since we were at a point of transition with the climb, we decided I could take a couple of days. We planned to put up the Bogus* first pitch on Friday, so I would leave for L.A. Saturday evening, after the Sabbath was over. We racked up that evening for the Bogus Start and went to bed.

Breakfast early Friday was another cold, dew-drenched experience. We were eager to get going on the actual climbing of the route again. We hiked up to the base, and I prepared to lead. My ankle seemed much better.

A short but interesting effort got me halfway up the dihedral (which we later found out is the route known as "Captain Crunch," made by Tony Yaniro and Paul Vance).

I reached a little pillar on the edge of the dihedral and got on top of it. Now off of Captain Crunch and into first-ascent climbing again, I looked to my right and could see the right-facing dihedral that I planned to pendulum into. Once there, I planned to set up the first belay. After I planted a bolt as high as I could reach from the pillar I was standing on, Mark lowered me down for the pendulum.

The pendulum was intense! Many tries and much chalk later, I stood up on the small ledge I had been shooting for. I was at the

---

* We considered this alternate start "bogus" because it didn't involve the high-quality, technical hooking that had marked the original start.

first belay of the Bogus Start. The rope ran almost horizontal from the pendulum bolt to my waist!

As I pounded on the drill, I had lots of time to think about what might become of things. I was curious about how all our work would end up. Would we finally make this climb?

As we fixed the ropes and rappelled to the ground, I wondered how long this pitch would stay fixed.

When we got to the ground it was mid-afternoon, and Mark had already stashed our gear in the woods, so we started back to the car. We had high hopes. We might be on the wall by next week—if we weren't stopped.

That Sabbath went by as a usual Sabbath in the valley. Mark and I went our separate ways on hikes. This was the first Sabbath that we really felt like we were about to finally get off the ground.

That evening I left for Los Angeles. I spent Sunday through Tuesday there while the real story was unfolding back in the valley.

Waking up Sunday morning, Mark began wandering around, trying to locate somebody to belay him on the Bogus second pitch. Not an easy task, and definitely one that took a lot of nerve and patience. Mark would walk up to somebody who would eye him suspiciously, and say, "How's it going?"

"Pretty good. Hey, I need a belayer. What are you doing today?"

"What do you need a belayer on?" Eyes narrowing slightly—a look of recognition.

"Well, it's a new route and . . ."

"Hey! You're one of the Mad Bolters! Forget it! I'm not touching that trash route!"

"OK, well thanks anyway."

"Hey, thank yourself. Where's the other Mad Bolter? I hope nobody belays you on that. Why don't you guys just get out of this valley?"

Mark would quietly walk away—looking for that right person who hadn't heard of the route, or who hadn't formed negative opinions about it—a seemingly impossible task! Rumor quickly spread that one of the Mad Bolters was looking for a belayer for the "trash route."

Mark meandered on. The scene repeated itself again and again, with variations. Finally, in the afternoon, it became obvious that nobody was going to do it that day. Mark decided to get at least a load to the base of the climb.

He loaded his pack with our portaledges and the last of our miscellaneous climbing gear—another 60-pound pack. He walked down the road a few miles to the trail, then up the trail to the base of the wall, enduring the constant harassment of the mosquitos. He finally stashed the gear in the woods—aware that any gleam visible from the trail could cost us thousands of dollars.

He stared up the shining, inaccessible slab, up at the fixed lines, then past them to the Overseer. He wondered if the slab would ever become accessible to us.

Mark headed down the trail, yet again, back to camp in the evening shadows. He ate alone, tried again to find a partner for the morning and finally went to bed, alone and discouraged.

All the next day Mark dealt with ranger red tape. Some of the rangers seemingly revolted against the "official" decision about us and our climb. Our camping rates went up and down twice during the course of the day. A ranger meeting was held to determine finally whether we would be allowed to continue the route. John Daley finally relayed the decision to Mark. Our camping rates would remain what congress mandated, and we would be allowed to proceed with the route.

It was evening. Mark sat at the table and pondered: another day gone. Just then a new person, loaded down with equipment, wandered past the site. Hope springs eternal! Mark approached the new face.

"Hey, are you new in the valley?"

"Yeah. I'm from England."

One point in our favor.

"Have you heard about the new route going up on El Cap?"

"No."

A major point in our favor!

"Are you doing anything tomorrow? I need a belayer for the day."

"No, what's the route?"

The needed opening. Mark launched into an awe-inspiring tale designed to incite sympathy and motivation in the poor guy's mind.

He bought it. First day in the valley, and the poor guy falls in with the ascent, unwittingly branding himself as being in league with the dreaded Mad Bolters, transgressors of all that is sacred, while knowing nothing of the "rape" he will help perpetrate. So Mark met "Mic." They arranged to meet again the next morning. Mark went to bed. Mic went to bed.

The morning arrived. Mic was not enlightened during the night. He was even enthusiastic to get started. They ate, loaded up some gear, and walked the few miles to the trailhead, then hiked to the base.

Mic was impressed by the forest full of haul bags. Mark dug out the racks, and the two climbers jumarred to the first belay. Mic got into a hammock and readied himself as Mark racked up. Mark tried to explain what was about to happen. Mic believed he understood. He was wrong.

Mark found a hook flake and hooked it with the typical Leeper narrow. It creaked . . . and held. Another hook and another. Some needed a little modification. Mark took the tip of the drill and leveled an edge out to better hold the hook. Or rather, to hold it at all. After five hooks, Mark drilled a bolt, rested, and moved on.

Hooking was a slow, tenacious business. The day wore on. Mic wondered what he had gotten himself into. He had never experienced a belay as long as this one. The hooking was, in his word, "Frightening."

Mark was four hooks out again, and reaching for the drill when, without warning, the hook pinged off. Mark racked up more flight time. The fall was a 30-foot, diagonal slider. Mic was vastly impressed and was doubled in laughter at the belay.

Mark reached the main seam in the original second pitch and moved up rapidly on copperheads. The sun set as Mark reached the hooking above the seam. A hook flake (it held weight last time) gave way and dropped Mark onto a rivet: yet another 20-foot fall.

A new rivet was drilled where there had been a hook flake.

However, a chopped rivet left a hookable hole, so one of the original rivets was not replaced. Finally, after a 14-hour day, by the light of the moon, Mark reached the second pitch belay. He was tired, yet elated. Once again, he was at our high point!

He fixed the ropes and rappelled down and over to Mic. They rappelled to the ground, stashed the gear, and walked back to camp by headlamp. Mark was in bed by midnight, without any dinner. He never saw Mic again.

The next day, June 2, Mark woke up very late. He had planned to move one more load to the base, but the stiffness and ache in his body quickly convinced him to take an easy day off.

He spent the day writing several long-overdue letters and reading. That evening I arrived and walked into camp to find Mark sitting at the table and eating. I joined him, and he explained the events of the past few days. I was impressed and flooded with enthusiasm. We would be on the wall soon.

We went to bed early. The next day we hoped to finally haul the bags onto the wall. We slept well.

On Our Way

The next day we drove to the trailhead, put on packs, and hiked up—yet again. I was thrilled when we arrived at the base of the wall. I'd forgotten how good two fixed pitches could look. We dumped our packs at the start of the first pitch. Then, battling mosquitos, we started lowering our haul bags out of the trees.

We moved loads uphill 100 yards to the start of the Bogus first pitch, until three haul bags of food and water were scattered all over. We made haul bags by taking two canvas duffel bags and putting an Ensolite brand pad between them. We hoped that the canvas would withstand the abrasion of being hauled up the slab. Once we made it to the Overseer, we knew that the haul bags would survive, since they would be hanging free in the air.

Two haul bags were for food; one for each of us. They weighed approximately 130 pounds apiece. We packed them very carefully. The edge of a can rubbing against the rock for even a few feet would wear a hole through both layers of canvas and the Ensolite pad.

Next we packed one bag full of Mark's water. It weighed approximately 150 pounds, and it didn't even contain *all* his water. We would have to put about seven bottles each into the gear haul bag.

While I jumarred up the first pitch and began to haul the three bags to the first belay, Mark lowered the rest of the bags out of the trees and moved loads up to the start of the original first pitch. After hauling the first three bags, I cleaned the second pitch, the pitch that had taken Mark until moonlight to lead. Meanwhile, Mark packed the other four haul bags.

I was suddenly filled with great joy. It was happening! We were finally hauling our bags onto the climb. Sure, they might still be cut down. But if they weren't, we were on our way. I was happy with the way Mark and I worked together. We made an excellent team. I thanked God for Mark.

By evening we had four bags at the second belay and three bags at the first. We were saddened about how the red mites that became crushed as we hauled up the bags had turned the sides of the haul bags orange. In the dim light, the clusters of haul bags looked unreal as they hung, casting long shadows.

On Friday, June 4, we took care of all our last-minute business on the valley floor. We considered leaving the ground for the big push, but decided that it was pointless to sit through the first Sabbath only two pitches up. We decided to leave the ground on Saturday night. That way we would rest through the Sabbath on the ground and spend our first full day on the wall as we climbed instead of sitting in portaledges.

We went to ranger headquarters to register for 30 days on the wall. This got us some very strange looks.

We gave Howard the radio he would be using to keep in touch with us. We arranged to have him call us at least three times a week. Twice on his days off, and once at some other point during the week. He said he would hike up to the base and yell at us when he was ready to talk to us on the radio.

It was important to have someone in touch with us, because we would need someone at the rim to help bring our gear down when the climb was finished, as well as collect any gear we would drop as we finished with it. Having someone watching us was also a major psychological boost. Howard could quickly facilitate help should we need it.

Saturday, June 5, we got up, ate late, and repacked the car with the remaining contents of our tents. By early afternoon everything we owned in the valley was either up on the wall or in my car. We drove over to Housekeeping Camp and took our last shower.

While standing under the water, I thought about the idea of not having any normal comforts for such a long time. I didn't know then how long the wall would actually take, and I couldn't comprehend what it would be like up there. I could only hope that I could handle it. I wasn't going to let myself get psyched out. After all the years of dreaming, the months of planning, and the weeks of struggling, I wasn't going to get up there and quit.

Mark was over in his shower stall and thinking the same things. Although he hadn't wanted the climb as long as I had, the past months, and especially the past weeks, had cemented his resolve. We were as ready as we were going to get.

On the shuttle we sat silently, not even looking at each other during the ride to the lodge. We got off and walked into Camp 4. One of the guys in our site gave us a ride to the trailhead, with the last of our personal items. We got out, shouldered the gear, and hiked into the forest.

Hiking along silently, we reached the talus slope. I was stepping from one rock to another, when the one under my left ankle turned under me. Instantly my ankle went out. The pain was unbelievable. Tears came to my eyes, and I collapsed in the talus. As the weight went off my ankle, I could feel it click back into joint. The pain slowly subsided.

Mark's eyes were wide. He said later that he had thought that it was "end of climb!" I sat for a while, white-faced, until the pain mostly went away then rotated my ankle. It was stiff, but not overly painful, so I stood up. It still didn't hurt too much, so I started hiking again—slowly. I realized I would just have to accept the fact that my ankle was unpredictable. It would just go out as it pleased.

I thought of Warren Harding's comment about how he and Dean Caldwell were the "March-of-Dimes Climbing Team" when they had spent their world-record 27 days on the "Wall of the Early Morning Light" of El Capitan. Mark and I certainly fit into that category. Mark had a knee that would go out on him the same way as my ankle. Oh well, we could at least empathize with each other's "trick" parts.

We reached the base of the climb. The haul bags and ropes were still up. This was it!

At 3:30 p.m., June 5, we left the ground for the last time. We

would not touch flat ground again until (a) the climb was finished,
(b) we were injured, or (c) the climbing became too drilled for us to
be able to rationalize continuing.

After moving our gear up from the first belay to the second and
organizing the bivy, we got out the portaledges and rain flies. We
spent about half an hour setting those up, mine on the right side of
the bivy, Mark's on the left.

The bivy looked good and functional. Seven haul bags in the
middle, and two portaledges dangling slightly below, one on each
side of the clump. An added benefit of the cluster of haul bags soon
became apparent. The bags formed a kind of ledge. Since all we
could foresee was one sling-belay after another, this was an
important bonus.

While we sat on the haul bags in the gathering dusk, the
realization overwhelmed us: "We are really here! We are actually
on our way."

I glanced at the rockscape as the light left the valley and we
finished our first meal on the wall. A party on Aquarian Wall was
rappelling from their day of rope fixing. The rock had an irides-
cence about it. The polished slab above us caught the last of the
light and glowed. The water trickling down looked like lava, on fire
from above.

I looked over at Mark. He was seeing it too! We sat in awe, two
tiny figures on a surrealistic landscape. We were aliens, hoping to
catch some glimpse of our capabilities and to become one with the
glory of the scene. Sitting on our rations, our security, and our
home for how long? The moment was magnificent as we were
stunned by the magnitude of our tininess.

Then the light faded away. The party from Aquarian started
their hike down the trail. As they walked underneath, they jeered at
us. We went down to our beds.

At this point, things went differently for each of us. My rain fly
had a door that I had designed. This meant that when I set up my
portaledge, I could cinch the rain fly tight underneath using straps
and buckles. Once that was done, I never had to deal with my rain
fly, until the day came to move camp up the wall. I could get into

my porty through the door in the side of its rain fly.

Mark, on the other hand, had no door. So when he wanted to get in or out of his porty, he had to squirm in between the rain fly and the portaledge frame from underneath. I found this process highly entertaining! Then he had to reach under his porty and pull a draw string tight in order to cinch up the fly around the bottom of the portaledge frame.

This involved considerable time and effort, especially in a wind. It was no fun standing in aiders and trying to get in between the porty and the rock, then in between the porty and the rain fly. Meanwhile, he had to try to keep the fly where it was supposed to be, as the updraft caused it to billow out like a hot air balloon. Finally, he had to roll over into his porty, at the same time keeping the fly in place as the porty frame went against the wall.

I had entered my porty easily and was snug in my sleeping bag, my safety line running out my door and up to the anchor. I listened to the flapping of material, the clanking of the frame, and the scraping of Mark's boots on the wall. The sounds grew increasingly funny as it became pitch black outside and as Mark's mumbling took on a frustrated intensity.

"This is such a pain! I can't get the rain fly where it's supposed to go! . . . OK! Finally, it goes around that corner, like I had designed it! I was wondering what its problem was."

Mark started to get inside, then stopped.

"Oh no! I'm on the wrong side of the strap! Oh! This is so ridiculous! I just can't believe it."

Mark got out his headlamp.

"OK, I'll play the game! If it's light I've got to have, then I'll have light!"

I heard more muffled mumbling from Mark's direction.

"All right, now, where is this headlamp cord going? Oh great! Wrapped around the strap!"

Light went out as Mark dealt with this new problem. I tried not to laugh out loud. Mark wouldn't have appreciated knowing how entertaining he was right then. The light went back on.

"OK now, up the aider. Now just stay where you are!" Mark

pleaded with the rain fly. He was almost in when a gust of updraft sent the rain fly straight up into the air, then dropped it back into Mark's lap in a heap.

Mark disintegrated into strings of epithets. "Am I never going to get to bed? This is just so unreasonable, I can't believe it!"

I was desperately trying to hold back any audible snickers, while at the same time, trying to sound as sympathetic as I really did feel. It was just so funny!

Finally, after about an hour of moans and groans, Mark settled in for the night. He suspected that I was doubled in laughter in my porty. However, he couldn't prove it until I told him after the climb.

We felt very strange that first night; almost alien, like we didn't really belong; like a child in a tent, sleeping in the backyard. Finally, sleep came.

I woke up in the morning to see my boots dangling above me. It was cold, and there was a lot of condensation on my rain fly. The sun wasn't due to hit our slab until after 11:00 a.m., so we had hours of cold to deal with.

We got dressed, and I put on my harness. Mark had slept in his harness. However, I had decided that I would be as comfortable at night as possible, so slept with just my swami belt. We put on our knee pads, gloves, sweaters, and parkas. It was cold out there!

I quickly climbed my aiders up to the anchor and settled down onto the haul bags, having secured everything in my porty and closed the door. I dug out a one-day bundle of food as Mark climbed up to the anchor. He found a comfortable spot beside me and dug into his food haul bag for a two-day bundle.

We ate, and the day was beautiful, crystal clear. We racked up while the updraft started and the line of sun crept toward our slab, moving across El Cap like a sundial. Mark put me on belay and settled back into a more comfortable position for the long day.

It took all day, using hooks, copperheads, and rivets, to climb about 70 feet above the belay. Most of the time I was looking at a long fall right into the anchor. I spent the whole day battling fear, forcing myself to use the features that the climb presented.

◆ ◆ ◆

At my slide shows I am frequently asked, "What would make you want to stand on those hooks? In fact, what would make you want to do such a climb at all?"

The answer to this question is complex. It has to do with reality. As we live our lives, we play many games: We do what we think we should, or what we think other people want us to, or what we think will portray the image we desire. Frequently we become so immersed in our games and masks that we lose sight of who we really are. Perhaps we become our masks and become what we portray—sometimes without realizing that we are changing.

Another factor is the sheer quantity of information that we have to process every day—billboards, full-color glossy magazine ads, TV programs, and radio broadcasts. No matter where you go, you are inundated by claims upon your attention. Other people have their expectations of you, and you are constantly urged to buy something.

As a Christian I have to keep in mind that all these external influences are temporary—they will all melt down when Jesus comes again. All the advertisements, with all the things I bought because of them, will end up swimming in the lake of fire. Other people's expectations of me will be meaningless as I stand before my Judge on that last day. The only thing that will matter then is who I have become. What kind of character do I possess? Is it such that it will be in harmony with heaven? Have I allowed Jesus to live in me?

I must frequently ask myself these questions so that I can maintain a proper perspective in this world. Yet the world places so many demands upon me that I often lose sight of these issues.

Often I feel the need to get on a climb, where things are simple and clear, where things are either black or white. Either the hook holds, or it doesn't. Either I placed the copperhead correctly, or I didn't. Either that rivet is going to hold the fall, or it isn't. The consequences of my actions are clearly seen in the Technicolor visions I have of what is about to happen if I blow it. I can see reality with an intense clarity on a climb. The usual trappings and facades that cover up the realities of life are stripped away.

When is the last time you looked at death and questioned your future fate? How yóu view your death deeply affects how you live your life.

What about your friends? Think about the games that people play with each other: telling each other what we think the other wants to hear; telling little lies so that we "don't hurt each other's feelings." Think about how we hide our true feelings. Think about how afraid we are that another person will discover a weakness in us. Think about how we protect ourselves from other people.

All these distractions are left on the ground. When I'm on a hook, it's very real. I can't hide from myself. I can't play any games to protect myself from my own self-examination. I'm laid bare, with all my shortcomings and weaknesses. I must come to grips with who I am. In fact, I must see myself very objectively—I have the opportunity to see myself as God sees me. I am forced to ask questions that demand answers. Other people's demands shrink in importance; God's demands become the primary focus. I find myself asking God, "Am I acceptable to You? Show me myself as You see me. Search my heart and show me myself. Show me my sins and shortcomings."

When I climb a wall, it is an intense search for reality, an earnest struggle to understand myself and to know God.

The morning of June 7 duplicated the previous morning. We awoke and dressed, but instead of climbing right out of the porties, we took care of another part of the morning routine. People always wonder about the mechanics of taking care of one's bodily functions on a wall. I will attempt to tastefully expose this whole affair.

(We found that the portaledges were excellent in providing privacy, both from each other and from the prying telescopes of the tourists on the ground. We used paper lunch bags to defecate in, while we squatted in our portaledges. Then we launched the bags to earth, to be cleaned up after the climb. We couldn't see hauling two people's excrement for 30 days up the wall. Also, we had less of an aversion to cleaning up later, after things had dried. The portaledges came to be known as "Potty-ledges" or "Potties.")

We ate and viewed the route. I was pleased with the previous day's climbing and was actually looking forward to getting on with the lead.

We noticed that the party on Aquarian Wall was going to make it to Timbuktu Towers today. They had gone for it yesterday, pulling up their fixed ropes. We didn't like having people above us because everything came down the slab. We were to like it even less as the day wore on.

I was already racked up, so I was leading by about 9:30 that morning. Around noon I reached a series of gashes in the wall formed by water and known as "solution pockets."

The second solution pocket extended horizontally about four feet and was about eight inches deep. It was filled with red mites and silverfish. As soon as my face reached the level of the slot, the silverfish tried to make me their new residence.

I hate silverfish and so began to do battle. They jumped all over me as I used my hammer to mash their bodies all over the wall. The little red mites were our friends, but they were in the wrong place at the wrong time. They, too, took their losses.

Soon the slot had smashed, gray carcasses all over it. Mixed with the carnage was red mite juice. The scene resembled a battlefield that had undergone heavy shelling. With the numbers of silverfish substantially reduced, I moved on.

The top half of the pitch turned into a rivet ladder because the rock became very rotten. Every time I tried a hook, it failed under less than body weight. I was deeply discouraged as I drilled rivet after rivet. Perhaps our critics were right. Perhaps this slab could not be done in decent style. If the next pitch turned out like this one, I knew I couldn't rationalize continuing. Yet the thought of lowering our bags back to the ground in defeat was too horrible! I tried not to think about it.

As I drilled, the party on Aquarian began yelling at us in a French accent to quit drilling and get off the slab. I wondered what a couple of foreigners cared about what happened here. They certainly didn't know the story. Well, they knew whatever Rescue Site told them. And it was turning out to be true on this pitch.

As I changed drill bits, an object whistled past my ear, narrowly missing me. It landed in the bivy below me, and I whirled to see if Mark was OK. He seemed to be trying to get out of the bivy. The Frenchmen were laughing and jeering from above us.

"Ha, ha! They take a direct hit amid ships. Ha, ha!"

"What happened Mark?" I was very worried.

"They dumped a bag full of crap on us!"

"What?"

The Frenchmen sounded like they were in orgasmic glee over their achievement.

The "bomb" burst open on one of the belay bolts and spewed its contents all over everything on Mark's side of the bivy. I was totally disgusted, and I wasn't even down there in it. I felt the anger rising in me.

The Frenchmen climbed on, and we heard no more from them. They couldn't wait to rim out and get back to Camp 4 to tell the Rescue boys about their aim, and how they had made the Mad Bolters grovel in it!

I had Mark tie me off to the anchor bolts so that he could deal with the mess he was in. I decided to continue drilling since I couldn't help him and since we still had to keep moving.

I moved up slowly as Mark fed me enough rope and then tied me off again to continue his work. I knew that Mark was at his limit of rage. After all, he was the one who was splattered with French feces. I was appalled but determined to maintain my cool.

Darkness filled the valley as I placed the belay bolts. After an hour and a half of work, I sunk the 3/8-inch bolt, anchored the ropes, and rappelled back to the bivy. I was famished and incredibly thirsty. Rock dust covered my face. I had decided to place the third anchor bolt the next day while Mark cleaned the pitch.

We talked as we ate. We had a lot to talk about: the "bomb," the bad rock, and where we would draw the line to go down. We decided that we wouldn't put up another pitch like this third one. Tomorrow it would be Mark's problem. The fourth pitch was his.

We went to bed exhausted. I had drilled 18 holes that day, and my hands were trashed. We slept like dead men.

CHAPTER 7

Breakfast in Bed

The strong updraft blew our ropes back and forth while Mark drilled the anchor bolts at the fourth anchor. It was evening, and shadows were snaking up the wall. The pitch had taken three days to lead. Mark's tapping on the drill sounded far, far away. I suddenly felt very alone. The feeling wasn't unpleasant, simply curious. Mark and I were isolated from the "real" world, and I was far from Mark.

The 1/4-inch bolt went in quickly, but the 3/8-inch bolt took more than an hour and a half to place. While he drilled, I grinned. The fourth pitch had not been over-drilled. There had been enough features to keep the rivet tally low.

The light faded as Mark finished the 3/8-inch bolt. He fixed the ropes to the two bolts and rappelled. We would plant the other 1/4-inch anchor bolt in the morning.

Inky blackness engulfed us as I reached the bivy, where I realized that I had been at the belay for more than 12 hours! My whole body was sore. Mark's headlamp flickered weirdly on the wall above, casting long shadows on the rippled granite and creating an eerie effect while the sound of his boots scraping the rock echoed in the night air.

The next day the sun reached us as I cleaned the fourth pitch, and Mark placed the third anchor bolt. I always looked down as I cleaned Mark's pitches and tried to imagine what the lead had been like. I would gauge the distance between drilled placements as I tried to find the flakes he had hooked. Mark did the same when he cleaned my pitches. This helped us rate each pitch.

We spent some hours at the upper anchor, organizing and racking gear for the fifth pitch. This looked like a traverse about 40 feet across the slab to the start of a seam, which I hoped would continue a long way up the slab.

Not wanting to start a traverse pitch in the early evening, we decided to rappel to the bivy and get ready for a relaxed Sabbath. As we rappelled, I began to get a glimpse of the scale of the wall. We were a long way above the bivy. The bivy was a long way off the ground. Yet we were not even halfway up the slab, and the top of the slab was only halfway to Thanksgiving Ledge. Thanksgiving Ledge was still some distance from the top. We had a long way to go! I began to feel like a mere speck, only marginally bigger than our friends the red mites.

At the bivy we sharpened drill bits for a while. We ate as we watched the swallows get their dinner. It was impressive to see their control in the air as the shadows lengthened.

When we retired to our porties, Mark mentioned that he didn't like swallows. It was clear that they didn't like him either.

The Sabbath dawned clear and cold. The granite shimmered with running water. The swallows swooped and dived for their breakfast. I slept through it all.

I awoke around 10:30 that morning. I realized that there was no need for me to have to get out of my warm sleeping bag. The air was still very cold. I watched a trickle of condensation trace its way down the inside of my rain fly. The sun wouldn't reach us for another half hour, so the drying wouldn't begin until then.

Finally, at about 11:00, Mark began to get up. The sun had reached around the Nose and touched our bivy. Things began to warm up. I could hear the rustlings and creakings as Mark maneuvered around in his tiny space. I decided to watch the condensation dry up. I opened my door to get better air flow through my porty. I wasn't going to be cold and wet this morning.

Mark wormed his way from under his rain fly and stepped into his aiders. I could hear his boots scraping the rock, then the rustling as he dug into his food haul bag. I peered out my door and looked up, but all I could see were the bottoms of haul bags and the blue sky. The sound of the plastic food bag was taking its toll.

"Man," I said, "I've got a problem!"

"Yeah?"

"Well, I told myself that I wasn't going to get up until the condensation dried from my fly."

"So?" Mark was unimpressed. "That's a problem?"

"Well, I'm really getting hungry, and the sound of your eating up there is causing me great pain!"

"That's a tough one, isn't it." Mark was still unimpressed. He resumed his chomping, switching to a granola bar, and loudly smacking his lips.

"I can tell that you really feel for me." I could sense the smirk on his face as I said it.

"Oh, you've got it rough. I can really see that all right!"

"Look at me, man! I'm getting emaciated!"

"Well, I guess it's just a matter of priorities isn't it?" This was said to the accompanying sound of a can of peaches being opened and a loud belch.

Things were getting serious in my stomach. "If you were really a good partner, you'd care about my condition because you'd know how much it affects you!"

Mark had an intuition about where this was headed. "Then I guess I should urge you to get up immediately!"

"But I'll get wet, and I told myself I wouldn't be getting wet this morning."

"What a decision, man! How do you decide which way to put on your harness in the morning?"

"Have pity, Mark."

"No way! To pity you I've got to sacrifice myself!"

"OK!" All pretentiousness aside. "So you see what I want?"

"Yeah, and forget it!"

"But, Mark, . . ."

"You're nuts, Rich. I'm not going to bring any food down to you!"

A long pause ensued while I tried to calculate how long the condensation would last on the inside of my tent fly, how long before my stomach would digest itself, and what tactic I could use to get Mark to relent and at least lower some food to me. If he'd just get me some food, I could spend the whole day without getting up, at least until I felt motivated.

I really wasn't all that desperate for food, but I didn't want to get up. I didn't need to get up, and I preferred not to get up—if I could just get some food.

The condensation wasn't even the real problem. It was just a ploy to cover the fact that I was warm and comfortable, and on this one day a week, I didn't want to have to be in slings when I could just relax, doze, and not worry about anything. The Sabbath was supposed to be a day of rest, after all!

I heard Mark making up a garbage bag to throw down. The situation was approaching a critical stage. If Mark started sharpening drill bits, who knew how long without food I might be?

"Mark?"

"Forget it, Rich!"

"Have mercy, buddy."

"Think of the work, Rich. I've got to clip and unclip 'biners to move over to your side of the bivy. I've got to clip into a long safety rope. I've got to climb down your aiders to get to you. Then I've got to climb back up and reverse the entire process to get back to my side of the bivy so that I can sharpen bits."

"I'd do it for you. It wouldn't be that bad."

"It would be less bad for you to get up."

"Mark, what a drag to get up! There's no reason to get up. If I just had some food, I could be in here all day. I could be comfortable for a whole day!" I had actually resigned myself to getting up. It wouldn't be all that bad. I'd just get dressed, get up, eat, and come back down for the rest of the day. The condensation was drying rapidly.

"You'll really owe me one!" Mark was wavering! He was empathizing with my plight.

I knew he'd seen the humor all along, but I hadn't expected him to see any seriousness in it. It really would be great to spend the day in bed. Even Mark could see that. Earlier he had said that he was going back down to his porty after he had eaten and sharpened bits.

"It would be a great favor—one I'd remember always!"

"Would you even lead one of my pitches?"

"Ha, forget it!"

"OK, then, suffer, . . . friend."

Wrong response, almost had it. "OK, let's negotiate."

"Then would you lead one of my pitches?"

"Well, I'll hold one of your falls."

"You've already held one of my falls, a whole bunch of them."

"Ha! Right I have. I've held some good ones too! You owe *me*, buddy. You remember our belaying policy: 'If the pain becomes too bad, drop the belay.' Right? I haven't dropped you yet. Right? I've suffered for you. Right? Then pay up!" I had him, I thought.

"Remember, Rich, you lead tomorrow!"

Uh-oh, I didn't have him. "OK, let's bail."

"What?"

"Let's bail. I thought you were my friend."

"OK, OK. I'll do it!" Mark was laughing.

A couple of minutes later, I could see Mark's boots coming down. A white bag was in his hand. My mouth watered. I was all set! Mark peered in as he handed over the bag.

"My, my, aren't we comfortable and lazy today?" He laughed at my hair, which was usually under a bandanna but now sticking out in all directions. I had gone a week without a shower.

"You're no beauty yourself, buddy!" I said to his ascending boots. Then I tore open the bag.

What a selection! We had done well in planning the menu. Cans of all kinds, gorp, granola bars, Pop-tarts, and Figurines. Cans of all kinds, what to eat now and what to save for supper? Hold it! No can opener!

"Hey, Mark! Where's the can opener?"

"Ha, ha, ha, ha, ha!" Mark's laughter said it all.

"Hey, most of this I can't eat without a can opener."

"Wow! That's a tough one, huh?"

"Mark, . . ."

"Enjoy, Rich, enjoy!" More derisive laughter from above.

OK! I started in on the stuff I could get at with fingers. Mark occasionally chuckled as he sharpened bits. Let him laugh. I ate and dozed off.

Around mid-afternoon I woke up again and decided to get up and at least look at the day. I clambered out of my porty, no condensation on my back today, and settled onto the haul bags. Just another day on the wall. Mark was down in his porty. I spent the afternoon just watching the birds. As the sun got low, Mark came up to eat. We watched as the sun went down, then went to bed. I was happy.

Two days later by early afternoon I had climbed up onto a low-angled ramp—and the point of decision. Where to plant the anchor?

Looking up and trying to see the next pitch from Mark's leading perspective, I could see what I thought was the start of a seam up on a steep, blank headwall to the right. The ramp I had reached extended to the left and up for about 100 feet. Although the ramp was lower angled and could be hooked, it stayed blank for as far as I could see. Two options—both having a certain merit. Yet, I had a bad feeling about the ramp, even though it would be the way I would want to go if I were leading it.

Since I didn't know what Mark would want to do, I decided to set up the belay at a point equally between our two options. Then Mark could choose. I was happy with the position of the belay because it was to the left of the water streak so we should be out of the water runoff.

While Mark cleaned the pitch, I drilled anchor bolts. After I planted four bolts, our new bivy anchor was ready. Anchoring the ropes, we rappelled down to our second pitch bivy. At the fifth belay, we had begun to feel that we were getting off the ground (650 feet up). Back at the second pitch bivy, however, we felt barely above the trees.

We had taken nine days to fix three pitches, and we still didn't know if we could actually move our whole camp three pitches in one day, as we had planned. We were way behind schedule. We went to bed feeling very low.

CHAPTER 8

We're Actually
Moving . . .?

Mark awakened me early on June 15 to say that it was 8:30 and that we needed to get moving. I got up into a gray sky. The air was still and cold; the stillness was unusual. Judging by the sky, we would not be warm all day. I met Mark on top of the bags to eat and to discuss our plan of attack for hauling 21 sack pitches that day.

Mark looked disgusted. "They got me again!"

"Who?"

"Those stupid swallows!"

It seemed that there was another bird dropping clinging to Mark's rain fly. This made five since the start of the climb! I hadn't suffered one yet. It did appear that the birds had a preference for bombing Mark. With each successive attack, Mark disliked the beautiful birds a little more. We speculated, as we ate, how much control they had over where their droppings ended up. Mark felt sure they had deadly accuracy.

After eating we got down to the business of dismantling our porties and packing the haul bags. The big hauling push had begun.

By mid-afternoon, we were more than halfway done. I had three bags at the fifth pitch anchor, and Mark had three at the fourth pitch anchor. I watched Mark below me as he hauled, and I realized that we were in limbo. Our home for the past nine days was no more, the anchor bolts weren't even visible any longer.

What home we had was in our haul bags. In that sense, we could set up our home anywhere. But we knew that we had to get everything up to the fifth belay, before we could set up anything permanently. The four-bolt anchor at the fifth belay provided the security and room needed to set up a well-organized bivy from which we could effectively continue the process we had affectionately named "Porta-siege."

Shadows crept up the wall as I hauled the last bag up and as Mark arrived at the bivy. He had more than 40 pounds of gear and ropes hanging on his body. We rearranged the haul bags to get the most frequently used ones on the outside.

Once the bags were situated and equalized between the bolts, we dug into the personal and sleeping system bag. Hungry and tired, we started setting up our porties. In the near darkness, we were aware that we had to be exceedingly careful.

Because we had to clip and unclip ourselves from certain bolts, slings, and ropes as we maneuvered around in the bivy, we were well aware that to clip into the wrong thing while unclipping from the right thing could result in a 650-foot plummet.

The cool evening air felt refreshing as I put my portaledge frame together and suspended it from my extender. Perhaps I would just beat the need for a headlamp. After clipping my rain fly to the extender and moving my portaledge inside of it, properly positioning the fly around the frame was easy because, with my door, I could see which side of my fly went where.

Once my porty was inside the fly and my fly was properly positioned, I lowered myself underneath to put all the straps through their corresponding buckles and tighten them. This process cinched my rain fly tight, so that I wouldn't have to deal with it again. I hauled myself back up to the haul bags and surveyed my system. The fly was tight, and the porty hung level from the extender. I was happy with it. I opened the door and began to throw my sleeping gear inside. After unrolling the Ensolite pad on the bottom of my porty, I spread my sleeping bag out on top of it. Finally, I threw the duffel bag containing my clothing on top of everything. I could crawl in at will. My porty was ready. I was home. I wanted to eat.

The bivy was still a mess, with slings, 'biners, and ropes hanging everywhere. But we knew we could organize in the morning; things were basically where they belonged. The main point was that we had broken down camp, moved it three pitches, and set it up again in one day.

Done eating, I went down to my porty. I spent a couple of moments adjusting my porty's suspension straps to get it just right. Then I crawled into my sleeping bag, slowly settled into a reclining position, and lost consciousness.

On the morning of June 16, I slowly pulled myself back to consciousness. Mark was telling me to wake up. *Why*, I asked myself, *is he always up first?* I knew that Mark hadn't gotten as much sleep as I had. I gave up trying to figure it out as I slowly and methodically went through the mechanics of getting up.

Cold, wet condensation ran down my back, despite my best efforts to avoid touching the rain fly. It was as effective as a cold morning shower. One cannot stay groggy with a wet rain fly clinging to one's back. Soon I was dressed and poking my head out the door. Mark was clambering out from under his rain fly. I suddenly realized that he could not avoid his wet rain fly in the morning. He had to have it all over him as he tried to get out from under it every morning.

Lead-gray, low-hanging clouds obscured from view some of the neighboring cliffs. The top third of Middle Cathedral Rock was missing in the clouds.

We ate on top of the haul bags and then stocked our porties with food and water in case it stormed. Another party below us was slowly working their way up Aquarian. One party after another seemed to want up that route.

After we had spent an hour of moving gear, slings, and ropes, the bivy was functional, with 11 ropes hanging down from the middle of the neatly clustered haul bags. We began to sharpen drill bits. This was an unending task. After drilling three holes, a drill bit grew dull enough to slow the drilling substantially. Since we had a limited supply of bits, we always had to stay on top of the situation. It took about 20 minutes to sharpen a bit properly. It took about an hour of drilling to dull it again.

The weather put on an impressive display. The clouds moved through the valley from west to east. Borne on invisible air currents, they snaked through the valley in white rivers, following the contours of the walls, rising and falling in the turbulence caused by the updrafts.

We discussed which way to go on the pitch above us. The guys beginning Aquarian Wall arrived at an anchor about 300 feet across from us as the party above us started their 14th pitch. Mark geared up for the sixth pitch. I put him on belay as he clipped his aiders into the leftmost bolt of the bivy. He had decided to angle left up the ramp. I tried to talk him out of it, but my only defense for trying the headwall was that it was just the way I felt it should go. My intuition on the matter did not impress him. He saw the low-angled ramp as the only sensible, logical way to go. I had to agree with him about that. We had to start getting farther left on the slab. The ramp seemed the perfect feature for that trend, yet I didn't like it.

As he stepped up in his aiders, the weather that had held back during our moving day finally let loose. Mark got out of his aiders and untied from the lead rope. We prepared to retreat to our porties.

Mark was directly above his porty so, by tying into his safety rope and lowering his aiders down, he was ready for a rapid descent to the comforts of his porty. He quickly got down to his porty and climbed underneath it to undo the draw cord of his rain fly.

I had other things to take care of before I could get out of the rain. I had to stow away my hammock, get my aiders resituated down to my porty, stash my rain gear, and move to my side of the bivy in order to climb down.

During this process I heard a giant boom! Mark thought it was just one of the jets that flew over the valley from time to time. I looked up and saw differently. I yelled to Mark, "Look out, something huge is coming down!"

Mark ducked under the haul bags for protection. I had nowhere to go as the behemoth approached. The party on Aquarian, far above us, had dropped a giant block. It had fallen free out of the overhangs and impacted the slab several hundred feet above us. Upon impact, it had fragmented into dozens of softball-sized chunks, and many, many smaller ones. However, the main mass had remained intact.

The main mass was about three or four feet square, and one and a half feet thick. This giant dinner plate, with its bevy of smaller buddies, came spinning down the slab right at us. I curled into the tightest ball possible. My head was tucked between my knees. I covered the back of my head with my arms, feeling incredibly exposed on top of the haul bags.

Out of the corner of my eye I saw the giant block go by us, making a terrifying whirring noise. It missed us by about 100 feet, struck the bottom of the slab with a ferocious boom, careened off the bottom of the slab, and launched itself into the forest, sheering off several small trees. Its velocity was tremendous, and the sounds of impact sent me into uncontrollable trembles.

Immediately after it passed, I curled into an even tighter ball as a bombardment of fist-sized chunks whizzed around me. As I heard them buzzing past like angry hornets, I suddenly realized that I was dead. With all the rock falling around me, it wouldn't all miss me. It would only take a golf ball-sized chunk to kill me. I felt a piece whiz within inches of my ear. I curled up even tighter, trying to reduce my surface area and protect my head. The hail of rock continued for perhaps four or five seconds, then slowly stopped.

I could barely breathe. Was it over? I didn't dare lift my head. My whole body itched with the feeling of the impending bone-crunching impact. Mark! I wondered if he was all right. *He was below the haul bags; he probably made it*, I thought. I was still unwilling to move.

"Rich! Are you OK?"

I couldn't talk because I was in such a tight ball.

"Hey, Richard! Are you all right?" Mark's voice reached a frantic pitch.

I heard him but was still unwilling to move. I slowly realized that it was over.

"Richard, if you're OK, say something!"

Mark, then certain that I had been hit, climbed up to see. I began unfolding from my tightly curled position.

"Mark, I'm OK. Are you OK?"

"Whew! Yeah, I'm fine. What took you so long to answer? I thought you had bought it!"

I explained the long silent period. We could not believe the size of the main rock or the quantity of smaller chunks that had followed. Mark said that from under the haul bags he could see rock flying all around us. He had realized that I was up there in the open and had expected me to get pegged. We couldn't believe I had come through unscathed.

I immediately thanked God for His protection even though I hadn't asked for it then. We called over to the two guys on Aquarian to see if they were OK. They had ducked under a small roof to avoid the flying chunks and affirmed that they were all right, although somewhat shaken up. The party above us yelled down that they were sorry and asked if we were OK. I yelled back that we were fine. Then we retreated to our porties as the rain continued.

I found that one of the rocks had penetrated my rain fly, right where my head would have been had I been in my porty. I pulled out my nylon repair tape and fixed the gash. Then I stripped off my wet clothes and climbed into my sleeping bag. I was cold, but not all my shivering was from the cold.

As we got warm in our sleeping bags, we discussed the sixth pitch. We quickly decided to go right, up the headwall, and get out from underneath Aquarian Wall as quickly as possible. We had endured enough falling objects from that route. We heard the party across from us beginning to retreat in the rain.

We could see that things were going a lot more slowly up the slab than we had expected and decided to begin a gentle food-rationing program. Nothing too drastic: just put away a couple of cans from each food bundle to save for a later date.

I spent the rest of the day listening to the small radio we had brought up. The rain came down all day, but we were warm and dry. The weather report was for intermittent storms for the next couple of days.

My main concern at that moment was the day-by-day, ever-increasing bend in one of the wooden joints in my portaledge frame. For the past few days the joint had even taken to making small, short creaks and cracking noises. I wondered about its integrity, but concluded that a one-inch-diameter oak dowel could not break under the minor strains that I put on it.

I listened to music until evening, ate a small meal, and went to sleep to the sound of rain. Yet another day on the wall had passed. Yet another night had begun.

CHAPTER 9

Of Swallows and Spiders

Sometime during the night the rain stopped, and many of the clouds moved away. I woke to Mark's telling me how much he was growing to hate the swallows. I lay there trying to get motivated and thinking about how Mark's battle with the birds began.

◆ ◆ ◆

Talking and listening to music until 4:00 a.m. convinced us to stay awake just a few more hours and get an early start on our proposed new route at the quarry. At the quarry we humped our gear up the talus, 100 yards, to the start of our chosen line.

Mark settled down to belay in a comfortable spot as I racked up to lead. By the time I started leading, we were both feeling the effects of no sleep. Mark grew increasingly drowsy as I led. The sun got high enough to reach us and made Mark's grogginess worse.

I was moving very slowly in an arch, feeling stupefied. Mark was dozing at the belay plate. The stage was set for a long, slow, lazy day.

Enter one misguided swallow.

To this day, we don't know how the bird got off course, but suddenly Mark was on his feet and dancing. I, feeling the tugs on the rope, looked down to see Mark feeding out rope as he danced backward on the talus. His arms were flapping, but he held onto the belay rope. Suddenly it was over, as quickly as it had started.

It seems that a swallow had flown, at full speed, right into Mark's crotch. Mark was instantly startled out of his drowsiness. The more Mark tried to get away from whatever was attacking his crotch, the more confused the bird grew about how to get away from Mark.

Finally, they parted company, and the bird flew away. Mark saw that it was a swallow and began to wonder about the malicious and unprovoked attack. Soon Mark began to distrust all swallows.

During other quarry climbs to follow, Mark was sensitive to the fact that the swallows dived at us as we climbed. They did seem to dive at Mark as he led. He learned to dislike them more and more. Then they began to try to land their droppings on him. I found the sight at a belay, Mark dodging swallows and occasional droppings, to be beyond hilarious.

I didn't know what to make of it. I couldn't believe that the swallows had singled out Mark. After all, there were a lot of swallows at the quarry, and they did dive at both of us a lot. But Mark was convinced, and there was some evidence to suggest that they liked him less than me.

♦ ♦ ♦

Now on El Cap the swallows had landed their seventh dropping on Mark's rain fly. I hadn't been hit yet. Score: Swallows—7, Mark—0.

I got dressed and climbed out onto the haul bags. The air was cold and damp, but the sky was mostly clear. Nevertheless, remembering the weather reports, we restocked our porties with additional food and water.

I found a comfortable spot on the haul bags and settled down to put Mark on belay. He repeated the procedure of clipping aiders into the bolt. This time, however, into the rightmost bolt, intending to head right, up the headwall. We looked at each other and then up to the headwall. There was a tempting-looking seam about 40 feet up and to the right. We could see only about three feet of the seam. After that it disappeared into a low-angled section around a corner. Hoping that the seam continued up through the lower-angled area to the right, which we couldn't see, we decided that this seam was Mark's first goal.

The rock looked almost as bad as in the third pitch. That pitch had become a rivet ladder. Would this pitch, too, turn into one? I was feeling pretty dejected. Mark was really unhappy, having gone from the prospect of hooking or free climbing the relatively low-angled ramp, to hooking up this steep and rotten headwall.

Mark stood poised on the bolt and strained to find a flake as the first clouds moved in from the west.

It was getting colder again so I put on my parka while Mark scanned the situation. The clouds hung out in the west end of the valley.

Mark found an edge and began the slow, careful hooking procedure up the headwall. Out about 15 feet from the bivy, Mark put in a bolt for protection. Then he continued up and right, aiming for the start of the seam. I heard a yell from below; Howard wanted to talk on the radio. I switched it on and explained our progress to Howard. He said that people thought we were going to the top of the slab where we would bail or take Horse Chute to the rim. One rumor was: "A thousand bolts to Horse Chute."

We responded that we were going to rim out, and it wasn't going to be on Horse Chute either!

Howard said that he would get in touch with us again on Monday of the next week. However, this was the last we heard from Howard while we were on the wall.

It was afternoon as Mark planted the first head in the seam. I was getting tired and uncomfortable. I shifted my position for the umpteenth time and popped a lemon drop into my mouth. The clouds were moving in on us again. The headwall had not been nearly as rotten as it had looked. There were some assorted flakes that were decent. These had enabled Mark to advance with only a couple of drilled placements, so the headwall had turned out to be a very impressive asset to the route.

Mark stood up on the copperhead and got his first look at the pitch above. He gave out a happy whoop. "Rich, it looks good. You were right about going this way."

"What is it, Mark?" I was instantly enthusiastic.

"It's a crack! Not a seam but a crack! You know, drive pins, slot nuts, shove friends—a real live crack!"

"Fantastic, Mark! What a break! How far are you from it?"

"Well, this seam I'm in is junk! It goes for about five feet, but to my left and up is a solution pocket. It gets a lot lower-angled up here. I may be able to go free up here in about 20 feet. There are scallops. There are cracks. There are . . ." Mark was babbling.

"Hold it! Hold it! How far to the crack?"

"Oh, I'd say about 30 feet, but I'll get there OK!"

"Fantastic! I had a feeling about this pitch—but what could I say?"

"Well, you were right. What a break!"

Mark mumbled on happily as he moved up the seam. Even a bad seam looked good after hooking. My mood improved dramatically.

Mark moved up quickly until late afternoon, when the rain started again. I lowered Mark back to the belay, and we went to bed.

The new day found Mark back up at his high point. I was, as usual, trying to find that totally comfortable spot at the belay, which just could not be found. I was quite chilly, even in sweater and parka, as Mark climbed on.

The swallows swooped and dived through the clouds. It looked fantastic to see them launch out from the wall and streak out over the valley like little fighter jets. From the front or the rear, they had the profile of a jet.

Layers of mist engulfed us for a while, then moved on. I felt as though I were a million feet up in the air as clouds of mist swirled around us in uneven layers. It was very entertaining as I watched the streamers of fog move through the valley, with the swallows diving through it all.

We had learned to watch the swallows to tell when it was about to rain. They seemed to be able to detect minute changes in the humidity. When they disappeared from the sky, I knew that either a peregrine falcon was overhead or it was about to rain.

Mark moved slowly and methodically up the crack. Suddenly two things happened simultaneously: The swallows disappeared, and Mark reached a place in the crack that was a silverfish haven.

I sent Mark's rain gear up to him. I knew that the rain was about to cut loose. While he put on his rain gear, the silverfish swarmed him. Then it began to pour impressive torrents of rain. Fortunately, because we had been warned by the swallows, we were already in rain gear, so we stayed relatively dry.

Meanwhile, the silverfish were literally crawling all over Mark. The crack was running with water since it was in the main water streak on the slab. Because their home was awash in running water, the silverfish made Mark their portable shelter.

Mark didn't appreciate the honor of it all. He couldn't understand how blessed he was to be their chosen one. Instead, he became their executioner. He started raining hammer blows in all directions.

Soon mashed bodies were everywhere. The rain washed them away, to make room for more. After about five minutes, the slaughter had produced many carcasses, but the number of silverfish was still overpowering. Mark realized that he was about to be overcome. Time to "get outta Dodge."

The higher he got, the fewer silverfish swarmed him. Mark finally settled down on a copperhead to get the last of the silverfish off his body. The problem was that they were all through his clothes. In the pouring rain Mark couldn't effectively get them all out of his layers of clothing. This was really frustrating because it meant that he would take them into his portaledge.

I was slowly but surely getting wet as I sat on the haul bags. The only thing that made it bearable was the incredible display of weather in the valley. The ribbons of cloud meandered through the valley, slithering like huge snakes between the walls. Sometimes the treetops would just poke through and give the snakes texture along their backs.

Mark decided to plant a bolt and then rappel. Placing the bolt was not easy. As he drilled, water ran down the rock, down the drill bit, and into the hole. The result was a slimy mud-pack at the bottom of the hole, which made for really frustrating jam-ups! Finally, after about an hour of work, Mark got the bolt in, clipped into the bolt, and created an anchor with it and a couple of lower placements. He quickly rappelled the haul line to the bivy, while I got ready to bail into my porty. We wondered where our buddies, the red mites, went when it rained.

It was about 1:00 p.m. as we got down to our porties. Stripping off my rain gear, I ducked into the door of my fly. I hung my rain gear outside the door and sat back into my porty to the overpowering sense that I wasn't alone.

Sitting on my sleeping bag, staring at me in defiance, was a huge wolf spider. This guy's body must have been an inch in diameter. I've never seen such a huge spider, short of a tarantula. He figured that he had found a nice dry place, and he wasn't moving! I moved my hand at him. He didn't back off, but merely crouched down to spring at me. I couldn't believe that he refused to be intimidated by my superior size and strength. This was disturbing.

I guessed that he was used to being the biggest, baddest dude on the side of El Cap! I didn't want to snuff him; I figured that he probably munched silverfish. But I wasn't going to share my space with the big, ugly beast with six eyes.

All six of his eyes stared up at me as I raised a shoe to crush him on my sleeping bag. I brought my shoe down with great force, then pulled it up to clean up the mess. Surprise! No spider, no guts, no sign of him anywhere.

Great! Now I didn't have the slightest idea where he was. I wondered how bad a bite he could inflict. He certainly had reason to be unhappy with me. Here he was, minding his own business, being warm and dry. Suddenly this big ugly brute, with only two eyes, tries to smudge him. I tried to communicate telepathically with the spider to tell him that Mark's portaledge was nearby and presently unoccupied. Also, Mark was bringing in a fresh load of food!

Mark, meanwhile, was having his own problems. He had lowered his aiders down to his porty and stood in one aider with one foot, not in all that stable of a position.

Suddenly I heard a scrape, a yell, and banging, as Mark's porty rammed into mine. Mark had reached under his porty to loosen his draw cord. On the wet, polished rock, his feet had slipped sideways, and he had fallen out of his aiders. As he went over, his foot stayed caught in the aider. He grabbed his draw cord as he went. Since his foot had stayed in the aider, he had been flipped upside down on the wet rock. He had ripped his draw cord loose from the corner of his rain fly as he went by. After a five-foot fall in the upside down position, his safety rope had caught him.

It poured rain. Mark hung upside down, staring down 650 feet of wet slab. He held a six-foot section of slack draw cord. His porty was rammed over into mine. Mark was really mad! He hauled himself back up into his aiders while I joked with him about his affinity for the upside-down fall.

"Hey! I don't want to hear it, Rich!"

This doubled me up, as Mark finally got into his porty. I left him alone because I did have a certain sympathy for him. Besides, I still had a huge spider to locate before I could feel secure. Mark got in some good chuckles of his own as I tore up my porty looking for the six-eyed monster.

I never did find the big guy. So I climbed into my sleeping bag, hoping he had gone to look for a better place to keep dry—like Mark's porty. There would be silverfish in there for him. I listened to the radio for a while then, as the rain pelted my tent fly, I drifted off to sleep.

I suddenly awoke about 4:00 a.m. The joint of my porty frame made very loud cracking noises! I sat up to look at it when suddenly it collapsed.

I freaked out. I had to get my weight off the frame before the dowel completely sheared in two. I tried to locate my glasses. After a search, I found them and put them on, but they didn't help. It was pitch black. Fortunately, the rain had stopped.

I stood up, clipped my swami off to the center support sling of the porty, and leaned off it to get dressed. My weight was now off the frame, although my swami dug into my sides as I pulled my pants and harness on.

As soon as possible, I switched my weight to my harness. Now I was in a little more comfort, which freed my awareness so I could experience how cold the rain fly was as it stuck to my bare back!

Mark was awakened by my thrashing around. He did well to stifle his snickers, although one did creep out every now and then. I finished dressing in the dark and unzipped my door. I expected a solid cloud cover. What would I do in the rain?

The sky was clear. I couldn't believe my good fortune. I could hammock outside. I climbed my aiders to the haul bags and dug out my hammock. I clipped it to the center support sling at the apex of my extender. Then I put my sleeping gear into my hammock, well aware that to drop my sleeping bag would relegate me to misery for the rest of the climb. I clipped one end of a sling to my sleeping bag and clipped the other end to a strap of my hammock. Now my bag couldn't go anywhere.

I boarded my hammock much as one enters a canoe and carefully climbed into my sleeping bag. This was not an easy process. When you're in a hammock, you have nothing solid to press against in order to move around. Getting into a sleeping bag, while in a hammock, requires you to move like a snake shedding its skin. Only you have to slither into your skin, instead of out of it.

Mark was silently cracking up in the comfort of his porty. I was worried. I hoped that I could fix the joint of my porty in the morning, because I didn't want to finish the rest of the climb from a hammock. I stared up at the stars for a while. Then I took off my glasses and put them into my hammock stuff sack. I couldn't solve the problem in the night; might as well get some sleep.

Around 7:00 in the morning the light in the sky woke me up. Mark woke up and joked with me about how this was the first day that I had wanted to get up before he did.

Mark climbed out of his porty and joined me in the clear blue sky. We discussed the fix. Mark was willing to donate the removable leg of his extender. We had built our extenders differently. My extender was a single, collapsible unit. It could not be butchered. Mark's, however, had one adjustable leg that could be removed. Mark's extender was destined to become an amputee.

Surgery on my porty lasted one and a half hours. The end result was a usable, but non-collapsible joint. I had taped the extender leg into a position alongside the broken joint like a splint. In order to run the tape around the porty's frame, I'd had to cut the fabric of the floor in five spots. This process probably substantially weakened the fabric in that area. Time would tell about that.

Since the porty frame was tubular, and the extender leg was tubular, they tried to go different directions when the porty was weighted. However, by playing with the porty's support slings, I was able to alleviate much of the rotation. The fix was effected, but not necessarily effective.

We spent the rest of the Sabbath drying out all our wet items and relaxing. While lying in my porty all day, I found that, although the splint rotated quite a bit, the joint sagged but did not collapse. Now my big concern was the fabric of the floor.

I slept fitfully that night, and I woke up occasionally to check the integrity of my repair. The extender leg had rotated to a point, but no farther. The joint sagged to a point, but no farther. If things continued this way, my porty might make it after all.

The next morning was our fifteenth day on the wall! Even with rationing, we would only have a few days' worth of food beyond 30 days. At our present rate of climbing, we estimated a 50-day route!

Mark's rain fly had been pegged by yet another bird dropping. Score: Swallows—8, Mark—0! We could not believe that I had not yet been hit. They *did* prefer Mark's rain fly to mine. Why? I couldn't even speculate. Mark shook his fist at the birds as they flew around getting breakfast. They were collecting more ammunition for Mark's rain fly. Mark vowed several types of terrible revenge! One involved a freon-powered, thousand-shot, automatic BB rifle. Because of my laughter I could not eat and listen to him at the same time.

The day dragged on uneventfully while Mark free-climbed up to a large copperhead seam and planted a three-bolt anchor. Meanwhile, I watched our buddies, the red mites. What did they eat? Where did they go when it rained? Who were their enemies? Could they communicate with each other? Did they comprehend their tininess on the vast bulk of El Capitan?

As hours passed I became more and more brain-dead. In

attempts to relieve my stuporous state I turned to one of our favorite belay-time activities: red mite teleportation. The concept is simple. You reach your finger down onto the rock. A red mite climbs onto your fingertip. Now he is yours; you must name him. OK, he's Herman. Next you take Herman and place him on an empty water bottle. Herman has never seen plastic before; he's in a whole new universe! Now you observe Herman's behavior—with the strictest scientific objectivity, of course. Herman runs all around the outside of the bottle, feelers going wild, and finally climbs back onto the rock; time to teleport a new mite. Reach the finger down. This next one goes onto an anchor sling. He's never seen nylon before . . . This goes on all day.

One of the things that amused me the most about the mites was their manner of handling a confrontation between themselves. Two of the little mites would approach each other from opposite directions. They would meet face to face. Suddenly, one would crawl over the top of the other, and they would continue along in their previously established directions. No big deal to them! They didn't seem to take even a second to figure out who would go over the top and who would get walked on.

Assuming an insect's mentality, you have to wonder at how they can arrive at such a momentous decision as who will assume the subservient position. I never saw them struggle for dominance. It just seemed to be already decided who was boss. One would squat, and the other would walk on him. Although sometimes they would go around each other, just as often they would display this peculiar behavior.

We spent a great deal of time pondering the little red mites. They were friendly, interesting little creatures, and we hated to crush them to orange juice as we hauled our bags up the slab.

Eventually, Mark called for me to come up and clean the pitch. Struggling out of my reticent state, I started up the pitch.

The belay was situated on a very steep section of wall, with rippled rock in all directions. We had reached a band of vertical wall. It was strangely oppressive to find, in the middle of the slab, all this blank steepness! The only line of weakness was up the water chute.

I was less than pleased with the prospects of my upcoming pitch. As I cleaned Mark's pitch, I planned where I would go with mine.

It was evening by the time I finished the clean. Mark could read the unhappiness in my eyes.

"Just doesn't let up, does it, Rich?"

"Mark, this is just so bogus, I can't believe it! Where am I supposed to go? You know—pick a blank spot and drill!"

I stared around for a while, until we had to retreat in the face of coming darkness. I had a sick feeling about the whole thing. I mumbled to myself, "Why do I keep getting the steep, blank, rotten pitches?" The wall was so steep that from the sixth belay, we couldn't even see the Overseer Roof!

We rappelled to the bivy in poor spirits. We had hoped for easier climbing on which we could make better time. I determined that, somehow, I would have to put up the seventh pitch in two days. We couldn't take any more time. Mark's pitch had taken four days, including the rain and the Sabbath.

We were way behind schedule, and the next pitch looked like slow going. My porty was crippled. We had no idea how hard it would be to haul. Would I have to jumar with it strapped to my back? I winced at the thought.

We ate in silence. We both felt very oppressed with the time this route was going to take us. I was determined to make good time on the seventh pitch but, as I went to bed, I was very aware that the difficulties could beat me back.

I lay in my crippled porty wondering—wondering. We would just have to stay up on the wall until it was finished. How long might that be?

CHAPTER 10

Casualty for the Swallow Team

The next morning we were up early to resolve the typical morning routines. Soon we were both up at the sixth-pitch bivy: Mark in hammock, and I leading the copperhead crack. There was a strong updraft the entire day, which kept my eyes streaming from the junk blown into them. The climbing never got nearly as hard as I had feared, although there was more blank than I would have liked: not as bad as the third-pitch, yet not as good as the fourth. Rappelling that evening, I was pleased with the day: 100 feet of climbing.

By the next afternoon I was at the top of the pitch. As I drilled the anchor bolts, I looked around me. Things were looking better. I had done the pitch in two days. We were finally out of the bulges. It appeared that it would take only about two more pitches to the top of the slab. We had thought it might be three or more! It felt great to look straight up the slab to the Overseer.

After two hours of work, I managed to drill out the 3/8-inch hole and plant the big bolt. I yelled down to tell Mark that I was off belay, that the ropes were anchored, and that he could clean the pitch. A couple of minutes later, I felt the lead rope tighten up. Mark was on his way up.

Mark slowly made his way up the pitch, his smile getting bigger and bigger as he saw the position we occupied. Finally, it seemed that we were getting up the slab. We were in good spirits as we started the rappel back to the bivy.

At the bivy our meal was almost a celebration. Somehow, being out of the bulges and being able to see straight up the last of the slab gave us fresh incentive to stay on our route.

We climbed down into our porties. As I drifted off to sleep, I had only one big worry: the head of my hammer was loosening on its shaft. I wondered how long before the head would just fall off. The constant pounding was taking its toll.

I decided that in the morning I would pound a RURP into the top of the shaft as a wedge. I figured that if I bent the RURP back and forth, it would break off in the middle, and I could drive it on into the shaft with the chisel. If the theory worked, my problem would be solved.

Wednesday, July 23, got Mark started up the eighth pitch. The RURP I had pounded into the shaft of my hammer seemed to have tightened things up. I spent the day hanging in my hammock and sucking on lemon drops. Having grown used to the long belays, I had learned to enjoy the hours of thought and looking at the little mites, the swallows, and, always, the beautiful sweeping wall. We had wondered if we would go crazy hanging up here for so long. I saw that I wouldn't. The sterile environment was very conducive to deep thought. I enjoyed the solitude.

Early in the evening Mark pulled up onto a ledge that we had hoped would provide a good bivy. We had seen winter pictures that showed this ledge holding snow, so we had planned to find this a very comfortable spot. It wasn't. Mark called down to announce that the thing was sloped, narrow, and basically worthless for our purposes. We decided to bypass it and named it "The Pits," from the expression "It's the pits!" Mark set up some placements from which to lower, and I brought him back down to the seventh-pitch anchor. From there we rappelled back home.

On the morning of the 24th I again put Mark on belay and settled back into my hammock as Mark self-pulleyed his way back to The Pits.

At the right end, intermittent copperhead seams ascended a rotten, crumbly dihedral, which ended in a small pointed pillar. Four hours of very dangerous heading and hooking above The Pits got Mark out of the worst of it. Forty-five feet above The Pits and to the right of it, he stood on a rivet and looked for the best place to set the anchor.

The water runoff from the Overseer fell free to the slab and landed about 40 feet above, and to the left of Mark. Because of this, he decided to get us as far to the right as possible. The rock in the water streak was more rotten than the surrounding rock, and even in the early afternoon, the whole area was wet.

Mark traversed up and right about 15 feet on hooks and heads. Ten feet to the right of the running water, he placed the first 1/4-inch bolt of the eighth belay. He was in a great mood as he pounded on the drill holder. "One more pitch, Rich! One more pitch; and we're up the slab!"

I hoped so!

Eventually Mark called down that the anchor was ready and that the ropes were anchored. Then he went to work on the last 1/4-inch bolt while I prepared to clean the pitch. Once more the 3/8-inch bolt had taken almost two hours to place. It was late in the afternoon as I weighted the ropes to ascend to our new bivy.

When I got to The Pits, I hung on the ropes and stared. It was as bad as Mark had described. If anything, it was worse!

I continued cleaning as I climbed up the rotten dihedral. I was impressed with the risk involved in the top of the pitch and was very happy that none of Mark's placements had pulled. If one had, Mark would have been badly hurt. A fall onto The Pits could have deadly results.

On the morning of June 25 we were up and had the morning routine taken care of by 8:00 a.m. After eating, we tried to pack our porties. Immediately problems appeared. My porty wouldn't even come close to fitting into its stuff sack. Mark's wouldn't even fold up.

Apparently the constant wetness of the Faucet Bivy had caused the wooden dowels in the joints of Mark's porty to swell up so that he couldn't pull the tubes apart to fold the thing up.

A cold updraft was blowing, and we were getting frustrated with our problems. I finally decided just to stuff my porty into the haul bag and hope for the best, not daring to untape my broken joint.

Mark, meanwhile, tried to pull his joints apart by clipping one end of a side tube to the anchor and lowering off to weight the other end by clipping his harness to it and bouncing.

Neither joint in the tube would budge. He tried the other side tube. It wouldn't budge either. It appeared that Mark would have to jumar with the huge elongated form strapped to his back. Mark was infuriated. I was sympathetic. I would have hated to have his problem. But I had others. Such as, would I have a usable porty after all the hauling?

We got the process into motion. I jumarred up to the sixth belay and prepared to haul my four bags up. I expected to be able to haul faster, since the bags would be substantially lighter, and this theory proved correct. That day was virtually identical to the one we had 10 days previous. Watching Mark jumar with the porty clanking around on his back was hysterically funny.

Finally by late afternoon everything was up at the eighth-pitch bivy. It looked like we were going to have plenty of time to organize before dark so we settled down on the haul bags to eat.

After eating, we set up our porties again, which was an easy task because they were both partially assembled. My porty had not suffered in the haul. The joint was still intact, and there was no abrasion to the porty's protruding parts.

By dark we were comfortable in our new homes. However, we were seeing major food problems. No matter what happened, it looked like we were going to be hungry at some point, and we decided to ration more severely while hoping that we could somehow speed up the climbing.

Sabbath I awoke to the realization that we were starting our 21st day on the wall. It seemed so unreal. I could hardly remember the beginning of the climb in May! The start of the wall seemed like a dream, and the position we occupied seemed like a fantasy.

I lay in bed wondering about the Overseer. What if there weren't good cracks up there? What if it was just overhanging copperhead seams? I pushed the questions out of my mind and started to get up.

We were high enough on the slab now that the sun didn't reach us until around noon. As we sat on our haul bags, we shivered as we ate. It was the end of June, yet we were still cold in sweaters and parkas!

Mark was peeved again. He had been pegged by yet two more bird droppings. Mark looked at me. His pained expression was comical. "Why do they hate me, Rich?"

"Well, they have known you don't like them ever since the quarry!"

"Rich, they don't fight fair! How can I do anything about their early morning raids?"

"Oh well, new score: Swallows—10, Mark—0! A big goose egg for you, Mark!"

The swallows swirled around in the morning air as I looked out over the valley. We were up high enough to see El Cap Meadow in its entirety. The sky was beautiful. The air smelled fresh. The meadow was green with pools of water dotting it. We could see cars and people down there. We felt so removed from their horizontal world.

I turned to the wall to watch the red mites scurrying around and again wondered what they did all day. What was their purpose in existing? Were they just some tiny part of a food chain? If so, whom did they feed? Did they have any comprehension of their tininess on this wall? Or was it just commonplace to be always scurrying around on the brink of a death drop?

I wanted to see what would happen if I knocked one loose and sent it tumbling down the slab. But I didn't have the heart. Would it slide and tumble until it hit a nickel-sized edge, a huge ledge from its perspective? Would it go all the way to the bottom, the equivalent of a million-foot fall for us? Would it be hurt, or would it just get up and scurry back onto the wall, sometimes climbing over the top of one of its kind, sometimes being the one to squat?

Mark had flicked a spider once, and the spider had fallen out of sight. It was funny because it would shoot out some silk, almost be brought to a stop, and then keep on falling. Either the silk broke under the impact force, or it came off of whatever was holding it. Had the spider gotten hurt by the fall? I wondered how resilient these creatures with external skeletons were.

Mark sharpened some drill bits for his lead the next day. I changed into my tennis shoes so that I could repair my boots. Even though it was the Sabbath, I figured that it was something that had to be done.

The toes of our aid boots had developed holes through the leather. I could feel the rock with my right big toe. Fortunately, we had foreseen the problem in time and, just before leaving the ground, had bought some quick-drying epoxy.

I pulled out the two tubes of the stuff and found a scrap of paper. I squeezed equal and liberal amounts from each tube onto the paper and, after thoroughly mixing it, spread the goop all over the toes of my boots. This formed a thick toe cap on both of them that would dry to a hard shell and, voilà, new toes to my boots.

I hoped my repair job would last for the rest of the climb because I'd had to save enough for Mark to do his boots too. If this epoxy cap didn't last? Well, the thought of standing in aiders in my tennis shoes was totally appalling! I hung my boots up to dry in the sun. Mark went down to his porty to get his tennis shoes, and I lazed back on the haul bags.

Suddenly I heard the sound of something big falling! The air whistled on the east side of the wall. I thought, *Oh no, not again!* and jumped up to look to my left. A large dark shape was hurtling down the vertical wall by Cosmos. It wasn't far away, but I could immediately see that it wouldn't come close to us. As I felt relief, I noticed that something was odd.

The shape was falling as fast as a rock, but too far away from the wall. As it covered hundreds of feet per second, it twisted and turned. No rock would make the contortions it was making. It was happening so fast. My mind boggled. What could it be?

Then I saw a smaller shape right in front of the big object. Two rocks? As they neared the trees at the bottom, I waited for the sound of impact. But then, unbelievably, the small shape disappeared and the big shape changed direction and skimmed out over the tops of the trees! The object gave a piercing cry—and it all fell into place. My heart raced. I had just seen a peregrine falcon pick a swallow out of midair. I had read that they could dive at 180 miles an hour, but I could never have envisioned the reality of it!

The speed of a swallow! Its maneuverability! I realized that I had just seen the master of the air! To be able to catch a swallow in mid-flight! I could hardly talk as I called Mark to come up to the haul bags, saddened that he had not been able to witness the spectacle.

I described the episode, to Mark's great delight! "That will teach them that they're not the hotshots they think they are!" The whole event made Mark very happy. He felt a real camaraderie for the falcons and decided that they would be a team. "Ha, ha! New score: Swallows—10, Mark—1!" But Mark had even more to say. "You swallows, listen! It may be 10 to 1, but my 1 beats your 10. I may have suffered your droppings, but you've suffered loss of life! You watch out when my friends are overhead! You may dump on my rain fly, but your bodies go to feed my teammates."

Mark loved it! The whole incident gave him fresh enthusiasm to carry on the mental battle. They were way behind, and they knew it! But most importantly, Mark knew it.

Mark got his boots fixed. We were ready for the next day's climbing. We watched the sunset and went to bed.

CHAPTER 11

The Cataclysm

On our twenty-second morning on the wall, Mark looked over at me as he stepped up onto the rightmost anchor bolt and said, "One last pitch of hooking, Rich, then I'm through with the real horror of this climb!" We hoped that he was right. Even A3 in the Overseer would seem easy if there were cracks.

After nearly 70 feet of climbing, with Mark at the top of a three-rivet ladder, it was well into the evening when he decided to lower off for the day. He was happy with the way that the pitch was shaping up. The last pitch of the slab would be a good one!

Mark was worried about only one thing. Higher up on the pitch was a deep crack that looked to be about 30-feet long. He had reason to believe (due to chirping and twittering sounds) that it was a giant swallows' nesting area, and his terror was mounting!

We ate dinner as we watched the sunset, which was quite spectacular since there was a substantial cloud cover moving in. We retired with food and water. It looked like we were in for a storm.

During the night a flash of lightning and clap of thunder awakened me. They occurred simultaneously. The electricity crackled all around us. The wind howled. Our rain flies fluttered violently. Rain poured down. I had never been in a torrent that hard before.

I was instantly freaked! Would our flies withstand the torture? Would we be hit by lightning? It was very cold, and I knew that we couldn't afford to get wet. I shined my headlamp around inside my rain fly and couldn't see any rips or leaks—yet. I lay back and tried to go back to sleep, but every time I started to drift off a new flash of lightning illuminated my cozy den, and the deafening clap of thunder awakened me. The lightning was striking right next to us. Not able to do anything else, I just lay there quietly, hoping that the storm would end soon. I could see that I wasn't going to get any more sleep that night.

It went on and on. Then around 1:00 a.m. I detected a new sound on my rain fly. In addition to the beat of the rain, I heard intermittent staccato bursts of . . . ? Were they big rain drops? Hail? Small rocks? I couldn't tell, but I didn't like it!

As the night progressed, the strange sound grew louder and more steady. Eventually it was a continuous deafening roar that seemed to be bouncing off my rain fly. I bundled my head in my parka, but most of the noise got through.

It was maddening, and I knew that Mark couldn't be sleeping through all this. So, I yelled over to him, "Mark, are you awake?"

"Yes! Oh man, Rich! Can you believe this?"

"Mark, I've never seen anything to match this!"

"What's that pounding noise?"

"Well, I've been thinking about it, all I can come up with is that it must be a . . ." I paused; the possibility was too horrible! ". . . a waterfall!"

"Oh no! If it gets any worse, it's going to just shred our flies!"

My rain fly was already beaten into a concave shape by the weight of water, despite the howling updraft.

We lapsed into silence as we thought about the waterfall. The rock above us overhung for 1,000 feet. The water must be falling free for hundreds of feet. We were directly below the bottom of Horse Chute.

The waterfall's pounding went on and on, accompanied by lightning and thunder! We felt terribly exposed. We were hanging out on the blank slab. The only thing between us and disaster was a thin layer of nylon. We knew that if we got wet in the biting cold, we would die of hypothermia and nobody would even know about it. Our sleeping bags were saving us, and only the rain flies were saving them.

The night went on and on. I could not sleep. Finally, some gray appeared in the blackness. The rain had not stopped once during the night. At least the waterfall didn't seem to be getting any bigger. I figured it to be a constant flow of about the same volume as someone pouring out a five-gallon bucket suddenly. As the day arrived and the waterfall continued, the grimness of our situation pressed in.

It was cold! Mark had pulled a bivy bag over his down-filled sleeping bag in an attempt to keep it dry. Condensation was trickling down our rain flies. Most of it was going outside the frames of our porties, but not all of it. Around noon I realized that the underside of my sleeping bag was getting wet.

The waterfall pounded. The lightning flashed. The thunder deafened us. Our tiny spaces seemed more and more cramped, yet they were the only safety in the face of death. My bag got wet enough to require action. I sat up to check the situation. I pulled my Ensolite pad back, which exposed a puddle on the floor of my porty. I moved into one end of my porty as it shifted around on the wet wall, and I tried to find a fork.

I tried to figure out where the water was coming from. I could detect no leaks, so far. Condensation? I found the fork and, pulling my pad out of the way, punched numerous holes into the fabric. As the water drained out, I stared silently at the butchered remains of my porty: the joint that was taped together, the slashes by the joint for the tape, the places that my rain fly had abraded on the rock, and (the newest desecration) the holes punched into the floor for drainage. It bore little resemblance to the new, good-looking porty that had left the ground weeks earlier.

I replaced the Ensolite pad and repositioned myself in the porty, which scraped on the wall to accommodate my shift of weight. Mark wondered what was going on, and as I explained my problem to him, his rain fly sprang a leak!

Mark stared up in horror as the first few drops landed on his bivy bag! It looked like the flies weren't going to make it after all. The leak wasn't bad, but it foretold bad things. Would we live through this storm after all? Mark positioned his rain jacket to catch the drips and funnel them outside of his porty's frame. A temporary solution at best!

I ate some food, though only a little; no way to know how long this would go on. Mark read part of a copy of the New Testament he had brought along. I turned on our portable radio.

The weather report was not encouraging: Rain was predicted for the next several days. How long could we endure? How long would our flies hold up under the constant beating?

I was glad that my sleeping bag was filled with Polarguard brand insulation. Even though most of the bottom side was wet, I stayed relatively warm. As the day went on, Mark's down-filled sleeping bag slowly lost its loft. His bivy bag wasn't letting all his body moisture escape. Mark realized that this was a timed game; once his bag lost its loft, he could expect to die of the cold.

Thus June 28 came and went. The rain didn't stop for even a moment. The waterfall was continuous. At least it didn't grow in volume. Slow torture; we were to be slowly ripped apart!

Night fell again, and with it an increased sense of doom. As I sat in the darkness, unable to see anything, the pounding noise seemed almost a part of me. Unable to push the noise away from me, to put it out onto the rain fly, I felt that my very self was being invaded by the overwhelming pressure of the sound. I tried to sleep, yet the storm continued, unabated in fury. I couldn't believe the intensity of it. Between the wind and the waterfall, I knew our flies couldn't take it much longer. The intense flapping of the rain fly made a noise that was only outdone by the roar of the waterfall. We yelled back and forth, trying to find humor in the situation, joking about bringing scuba gear on our next climb, if we lived through this one.

Around 1:00 a.m. I heard muffled shouting. Mark's porty began shifting around, and his headlamp came on. The light was a great relief in the oppressive darkness!

"What's going on, Mark?!"

"My porty is collapsing!"

"What?"

"My joint just broke!"

"What are you going to do?"

"I'm trying to find my hammock. I've got to get my weight off this thing!"

Mark, who was happy now that he always slept in his harness, clipped his harness to his center support 'biner. This got his weight off his porty frame. He was swimming in condensation as he tried to get his hammock out and set up, no easy feat, as he tried to avoid getting any wetter. At least he had brought his hammock into his porty. Intuition?

The goal: Get an Ensolite pad, a sleeping bag with bivy bag, and himself into the hammock. His hammock, clipped to the center support, hung limp. Mark could barely maneuver in the confines of his tiny space, and the wet rain fly clung to any part of his body that it touched.

With difficulty he got all his sleeping gear into the hammock. Now to get himself in between the proper support slings and into the hammock. There were six slings for the hammock and six for the porty. Twelve support slings. Which to go under, which to keep on one side, and which to keep on the other?

Mark's headlamp flickered in the darkness as he tried to get into the hammock without weighting his crippled porty frame, 1,100 feet in the air, all the time expecting something else to go wrong, some final thing that would spell disaster!

I felt his fear. What more could happen? Would things get worse? How much longer would the storm last?

After hours of effort and frustration, Mark got into his hammock and settled down to rest, but rest wouldn't come! The storm continued!

The morning of June 29 arrived, and I hadn't slept all night. My mind was getting fuzzy and dull. The constant stress and pounding was slowly driving me nuts. At least I was in a porty—for now. I pitied Mark in his hammock and wondered about my own porty's joints. The light of day at least enabled me to see my straining rain fly, which separated me from the waterfall. This helped me keep the noise "out there" because I could see where the noise came from. The storm continued unendingly through the day.

Finally, I began to feel beaten. I could see that we weren't actually going to make the route. This storm was the final setback. While there was daylight we should just get into our rain gear, collapse our porties, dismantle the anchor, drop all the junk to the ground, and bail off of the route. Because of the storm we could probably succeed with this and get out of the valley before anyone even noticed us missing.

No! My mind rebelled against quitting. *Just hang in there, Rich! Just concentrate on enduring this. It can't go on forever. Can it?* I continued my earnest prayers for strength and endurance.

I tried to sleep, but couldn't. The noise was unbelievable! Every time I started to tune out the constant pounding and drift off to sleep, a peal of thunder shocked me awake. A deep frustration set in. It was so oppressive! I could not eat because we were already rationing food, and storm days had to be considered lost days. I had no desire for even a sip of water. Water was all around, and I was far from thirsty.

The effort of yelling to talk with Mark soon made that an unreasonable proposition. Nothing was left for me to read; the only sanity lay in listening to the radio. The radio provided some measure of contact with a world that had not gone completely crazy and kept me hoping that the storm would pass. However, the weather reports were never encouraging. They spoke only of a solid cloud cover from the ocean, which was hundreds of miles away.

Tuesday came and went in the constant pounding of the waterfall! On the radio I heard that a foot of snow had dropped on the rim! In June? A new concern: Would chunks of ice be shot down our way with the waterfall? I could feel the cross hairs trained on me.

The waterfall continued through the night and into the next day. During the night, I fell into an exhausted sleep, which was fitful and interrupted by the lightning and thunder. On the morning of the thirtieth the rain stopped. Around 1:00 p.m. the waterfall slowed—and stopped. It was fearfully quiet.

We breathed silently, carefully, as if any sign that we had survived would start the torment again. Was it over? I opened my door and looked out. Solid overcast. Well, what to do? We conferred quietly and decided, somehow, that we wouldn't quit. We decided to repack our haul bags, readying them to dump some of our gear. We planned to dump our portaledges when we had the ninth pitch fixed. They were trashed anyway!

We climbed out and began reorganizing. For each of us, the sight of the other, sodden and pale, was encouraging yet disturbing. How much more could we have taken? The solid cloud cover made us wonder how much more was yet in store.

First, we figured up how much water we could possibly need to rim out. We dumped out all the extra. We put the empty bottles into an empty haul bag.

Next we packed six of our 11 ropes, knowing that we were going to lose them once they hit the ground and other climbers could get them. Oh well. They weighed eight pounds each, and we needed to dump that weight. We kept two lead ropes and three haul lines— one for each haul bag.

All our spare clothes, dirty clothes, and any nonessentials went into another bag. The fourth bag hung empty, awaiting our portaledges. We had consolidated everything we needed into three haul bags. After only three hours out of our porties, we returned to them because the rain had started again. At least it had held off long enough for us to accomplish something.

In the light rain, Mark fixed his broken porty joint with an ingenious setup involving a large hex and two drift pins. This got him out of his hammock, and back into his porty. Although not particularly happy with his repair job, his spirits were up again.

June 30 turned into night, and as the rain increased, the waterfall began again. We had resigned ourselves to patient endurance. We would ride it out. We would not give up!

Sometime during the night, the rain and waterfall stopped. I fell asleep! Thursday morning, the first of July, arrived with sunshine! I awoke to the sun on my fly. Sunshine! I couldn't believe it! I got up enthusiastically, feeling really hungry. We had eaten almost nothing during the storm, hoping to salvage our rationing program, and as I got dressed I looked forward to a "big" breakfast.

I met Mark on the haul bags, and we looked out over the valley. From our height the valley looked saturated. El Cap meadow was a huge lake; the rest of the valley, a marsh! I checked my rain fly from the outside. It seemed to be OK. I was suddenly overjoyed; we had survived! We would go on!

As we ate we discussed the realities of life, feeling that we could not afford another storm. Although, we really didn't know how much we could endure. I wondered how much we would suffer for this route. We hoped that our suffering wouldn't involve another storm!

The first order of the day was to dry out. Going down to my porty, I pulled out all my sleeping gear, unzipped my sleeping bag, and hung it along with my Ensolite pad to dry in the open air. My parka and wet clothes quickly followed.

Several hours later it was still cold. Drying would be an all-day affair. Mark checked on his porty joint repair as I teased him about the opportune time it had chosen to fail.

The storm had been a tremendous test of our resolve to stay on the climb. It seemed as though everything had conspired against our desire to succeed with our dream. Our spirits were torn between the desire, which was almost a need, to go back to the ground and our dream to ascend the wall. As the storm raged, the temptation to quit and get down was almost overwhelming. We wanted to quit so badly! Yet we wanted to climb that wall. The mental struggle between the two choices was so draining that exhaustion almost made the choice for us. "Why," we asked ourselves, "should we struggle against our natural desires to retreat?"

As I confront temptation, it is clear that I am a natural quitter. By myself I have no power to stand firm in the Christian life. Just as we deeply desired to quit in the face of our adversity, I frequently yearn to quit in the face of temptation. The desire to be a quitter will be with me as long as I live in this mortal body.

Not all temptations are cataclysmic. Christ had only one desert temptation experience and only one Gethsemane. Although His life was one of constant trial and temptation, only a few incidents appear to have really shaken Him to His core. Likewise, my life has many trials and temptations, yet God only allows the cataclysms on occasion and then only when He also provides the strength to endure them.

What decides the outcome when a storm of temptation assails me? (This applies even to the many small storms.) The decision is based upon very few things.

First, I must decide that the Christian life is truly beautiful, that Jesus is indeed the person I must want my life to reflect.

Next, I must determine to reach that goal. Although this seems almost simplistic, it is a fact that without my will being focused upon my goal, I waver in any breeze, let alone storm. When I unite my will with the power of Jesus Christ, He makes my will reality.

Finally, "Having done everything, to stand firm" (Eph. 6:13). Once points one and two are established, I am standing. I must then simply continue to stand firm, resisting natural impulse, seeing things from God's perspective, and enduring until God has tried me and brought me forth as gold.

This is the fight of faith: having faith that God will see me through, clinging to His promises that His grace is sufficient for me, and standing upon those promises. If I use this kind of faith, I cannot be moved. The climb continues!

Around 2:00 p.m. Mark tied into the lead rope. He self-pulleyed up to his high rivet as I pulled in the slack rope. Lead nine continued.

I looked down at El Cap meadows and thought about the storm. A foot of snow on the rim? How bad had it really gotten? Did we just squeak by without even knowing it? We knew that three teams had been rescued during the storm. I prayed for no more storms.

By early evening Mark reached the start of the large crack. It was, as he had feared, a huge swallows' nesting area! He decided to place a couple of friends and rappel for the night—before the swallows came out for their evening feeding.

Friday, July 2, was another clear, cold day. I wished it would warm up. I was really tired of being cold all the time. As we took care of the morning routine, we talked and realized that we both had come to the same conclusion: We were sick of the wall.

It was no longer fun. It was no longer new. We no longer enjoyed the routine. The whole thing had become a drudgery. We wanted to get off the wall and get back to some normal comforts such as showers, beds, and hot food. We wanted out of the world where not clipping everything in would result in embarrassment or disaster! We were tired of the endless insecurity and pain.

Mark jumarred up to his anchor and tied into the lead rope, yet again. I put him on belay, yet again. He looked up to scan the rock, yet again. I tried to find a comfortable spot, without success, yet again.

Mark started free-climbing the crack. It was quite easy, a real break. Suddenly Mark's worst nightmare came true. Disturbed swallows streamed out of the crack above him. Several birds hurtled straight at his face. This made the 5.7 crack a 5.10, as he was almost knocked over backward. I was helpless with laughter as the birds began a systematic attack.

Mark moved up quickly in the crack as the birds swirled around him, pecking and beating their wings at him. He was distressed when some of the birds hit him in the head as they went by. Mark looked down for sympathy—and found none.

"Ha, ha, ha! You're on your own, buddy! You brought this on yourself when you joined the falcon team!"

"But, but—I never knew they would retaliate like this! What am I supposed to do? I can hardly climb!"

"Strike a truce. Although, I doubt if they'll buy it. They've suffered too many desecrations by your hand already!"

"Desecration? By my hand? They bombed my rain fly again this morning! That makes 11. How many have you had? I'll tell you—*zero!* Who's suffering desecrations at whose hand? Wing? Whatever!"

"Well, I suggest that you move out! The longer you stay where you are, the worse you get it."

"I'm moving! I'm moving!"

Mark got up the crack quickly, if not easily, in spite of the fury of the birds' defense of their home. I couldn't stop laughing as Mark tried to get away. Unfortunately, he had to go out onto hooks above the crack. Hooking was bad enough without the birds! They almost knocked him out of his aiders time and time again.

Fortunately, as he got higher above their crack, their attacks lessened and finally stopped. Instead, they concentrated their attention on his lead rope and haul line. We wondered if they would somehow shred his ropes to pieces! Finally, they returned to their nests. All parties knew who had emerged victorious!

Mark, much relieved, hooked and rivetted up to the Horse Chute anchor. He clipped into the anchor bolts and plunged a couple of friends into the nearby arching crack. Soon Mark had a hauling system set up, so I sent the three bags out on their ropes. Mark hauled two of the bags while I cleaned the pitch. It was early afternoon when I reached the ninth anchor and watched Mark haul up the third bag.

Finished with the ninth pitch, we rappelled back to the bivy and dropped our excess baggage. Everything we needed for the rest of the climb was up at the ninth anchor. Only an empty haul bag hung waiting for our porties on Sunday.

It was uncomfortable to stand in slings (the ledge of haul bags we used to sit on was gone), so we crawled into our porties to eat. We had a minimal stock of food to get us through the Sabbath.

Mark worked on the joint of his porty again. It had sagged a little, so he repositioned the hexentric and pounded in the drift pins a little harder. By early evening we were asleep.

The Sabbath slowly passed. We savored the comfort of our portaledges. We would drop them tomorrow. Hammocks to the rim! We hoped fervently that we wouldn't have to endure another storm once we were in our hammocks.

What we couldn't see: the clouds moving in! Around 6:00 p.m. we were shocked to hear rain drops on our flies.

"Oh no, Mark! Here we go again!"

"I just can't believe this, Rich! When are we going to get up this route?"

The rain and wind increased in intensity, until around dark we heard the dreaded sound—the increasing dull roar of the waterfall. We resigned ourselves for the worst. We didn't know how long this storm would last. We didn't have much food in the porties, which was just as well, since there was no point in eating as long as we weren't moving up. We were, however, very happy not to be in hammocks.

Sometime during that night, it all quieted down. I slept anxiously, expecting to get it again any minute.

CHAPTER 12

Enter:
The Overseer

We woke up early the next morning. There was sunshine! We climbed out enthusiastically: not a cloud in the sky! We felt blessed and quickly got our morning routine taken care of.

I lowered down to undo my rain fly's straps. This done, I climbed back to the anchor, pulled up my rain fly, unclipped it from the anchor, put it away (to be hauled up with us), lowered back down, collapsed my porty completely, and stuffed it into the haul bag. Meanwhile, Mark was doing the same thing, only more quickly. He didn't have straps to deal with on his rain fly, and his porty frame still wouldn't collapse.

Soon both porties were in the haul bag. We gave them a last longing look and dropped them. As they fell, we wished we would have been able to use them in the overhangs, but in their crippled states, they would have absorbed too much of our time. When they hit, we knew we had to quit moping and move out.

We dismantled our anchor and jumarred to the ninth belay. The slab had taken 28 days. We had just broken the world record for the longest time anyone had lived continuously on a rock wall while climbing it, and we were only halfway up.

I spent the whole day leading the tenth pitch. It involved an overhanging slot that required our largest friends, hexes, and bongs to be placed straight up over my head as I traversed. Many times I had to stack friends against hexes in order to fill the huge crack. The slot was running with slime water in spots. I got coated!

Reaching the thinnest point of the roof, I placed a five-rivet ladder to reach the Overseer crack. We were finally in it! The crack was a good, deep A1 crack, with only one problem: It was filled and overgrown with a strip of growing turf—all the way out its length!

I had to dig the turf out of the way to expose the crack, put in a placement, stand on it, reach out, and continue gardening.

As soon as I had gotten up the five-rivet ladder, I was out of Mark's sight, so as I traversed the turf crack, which we named "Hanging Turf Gardens," all Mark could see of my progress was the rope slowly feeding out and the big chunks of turf falling to the slab.

The pile of dirt and turf piled up on The Pits. Sometimes a large turf-pack would hit the pile and knock most of it off. This made room for a new pile, as the old pile rained down to the ground, 1,000 feet lower, and formed another pile. As the day wore on, this process provided Mark's only entertainment.

My crack got harder as I got farther to the left. The crack was A3, and it was night by the time I reached the best spot for an anchor. By headlamp I placed a bunch of tied-off pins and set to work on some bolts. Since we could only place 1/4-inch bolts, I was glad that the belay was not on overhanging rock.

After placing three bolts, I anchored the ropes and began to haul the bags.

As I hauled, I could see Mark's headlamp flickering weirdly on the wall below, and I heard muffled grumbling as he cleaned.

It seemed that he couldn't see my placements and remove them at the same time. They were buried so far up in the slot that he had to put his face against the wall, into the running slime, in order to look up with his light to see them. But, in that position, he couldn't reach his hand up to get them. So he had to look up and form a mental picture of a placement, then reach up and feel around for it, and finally get his hammer up to remove it. All the while, slime ran out of the crack. Soon Mark was also coated.

I got the bags up and anchored before Mark arrived, leaving room for us to set up our hammocks. Mark was at the rivet ladder when I finally leaned back to relax for the first time that day.

Relaxation wouldn't come. Within the limited scope of my

headlamp light, I could see that we were anchored 1,200 feet up at the lip of the thickest part of the Overseer Roof. We were at the end of our first overhanging pitch. Above me the rock overhung wildly.

Mark was not impressed with the nighttime clean, and he hated to arrive at a new anchor at night.

Once Mark arrived, we set up our hammocks, crawled in, and went to sleep. It was 1:30 a.m.

During the night Mark woke up. Water dripped from the crack above him and landed on his face! Not wanting to get up and dig out his rain fly, he put his rain jacket over his head and went back to sleep. The drips were small, but irritating, and they continued all night.

A hammock is not a comfortable place to sleep so, as the sky began to get light, we woke up. We tried to go back to sleep, but couldn't. It was 6:00 a.m. We were still tired!

I pulled my hands out of my sleeping bag to rub my eyes. They were cramped! I stared at them, feeling betrayed. At least the cramping wasn't particularly painful; it was simply annoying. After some work I got them unlocked, although not really functional, and went ahead with rubbing my eyes. I looked up to see if what I had seen last night was true. Yes, the start of the next pitch, as far as I could see, was an overhanging copperhead seam!

"Mark?"

"Yeah!" Said from under his parka in muffled tones.

"We've got some problems."

"So. What else is new?"

"Ah, yeah. Well, we're almost out of copperheads, for one thing. Take a look up."

"Do I have to?"

"No, we could just bail from here quietly."

"OK." Mark pulled his head out from under his parka. "OK. What are you talking about? Oh! Oh no-o-o-o! This can't be! There are supposed to be A1 cracks up here!"

"Yeah, tell me about it. I think we may be in trouble, Mark!"

"OK. You're right, Rich. That's a problem. What are the rest of our problems, since you seem to be so well up on them?"

"Well, you're not going to like this one very much."

"Do I like *any* of them very much?"

"True! You don't. What a crummy attitude! Almost as bad as mine. Anyway, I'm not going to be able to lead, at least not right away today."

"What?"

"Well, my hands are totally locked up. They cramped up last night, and now they're only marginally functional."

"Rich, this is ridiculous!"

"Yeah, I know you don't want to lead. I'm not asking you to. I'm only saying that I'm not going to be able to just hop up and romp that copperhead seam. And once I do, we're going to be about out of copperheads. If the next part of the Overseer doesn't develop some good cracks, we're going to be in big trouble!"

"Well, we can't sit around here all day!"

"So, what do we do? I can't lead right now. I'm sorry. I'm not loving it either. I'd rather be able to use my hands! But maybe later on this morning I can go up. Let's eat and see what happens." We dug out some food and ate. We were down to about 1,500 calories per day. My hands refused to loosen up; they could barely hold the fork, so Mark was confronted with the choice.

He made it, and tied into the lead rope, stating clearly that he was unhappy and was only doing it so we could get moving.

With difficulty, I got the lead rope through the belay plate, and settled back to belay. At least I could hold the rope! I was good for something. I found the whole predicament to be quite embarrassing and frustrating. Mark spent the day maneuvering his way up the overhanging rock. The copperhead seam was not as bad as it had looked, but above it was worse than we had hoped.

Mark moved up on very shaky RURPs and copperheads all day. Nightfall found Mark up only half the pitch, so I had to lower him down to spend the night.

Soon he was across from me, at the same level, but 30 feet away and dangling 30 feet out from the rock as well! He hung there, slowly spinning, 1,200 feet off the ground and nowhere near anything to grab onto.

I anchored his haul line, and he used it to laboriously pull himself into our anchor. As he anchored himself, he mentioned his distaste for the way his lead rope ran through the bulges above. That settled that! Even though I could lead the next day, Mark would finish the lead he had started. I had no interest in jumarring a single line that I did not know the run of, especially after hearing Mark's comments.

Mark presented a new piece of long-awaited information, "Rich, it's worse than we had thought it would be up there!"

"Don't say it."

"Yup! Overhanging copperhead seams—all the way to the end of the Overseer Cracks!"

"Well, we're in deep trouble!"

"Look, Rich, if we don't have enough heads, we're going to have to drill a rivet ladder next to a usable crack, just to get up. I can't see doing that!"

"No way! We're not doing that! We may have to bail, but we're not drilling next to a crack!"

"Well, we can bail from here pretty easily. We just rappel down onto the slab and down we go. But once we're up there a pitch or two, we have to down-nail to get back to this anchor before we can rappel. You saw how far I was from the rock after being lowered only half a pitch!" (Rappelling in overhanging rock only deposits you out away from the wall. Being out of reach of the rock, you are unable to anchor yourself in for the next rappel. The only alternative is to down-nail, placing pitons, etc. in the crack as you go, which keeps you close to the wall. The last one down has to down climb the crack, actually down lead, in order to retrieve the gear.)

"Yeah, Mark, I know. We really commit once we leave this anchor! But I can't see going down. Not after so much work! We've got to rim out!"

We sat in silence for a while. Both of us had our doubts.

"Mark! We've got to go for it! If we don't make this route, we'll never forgive ourselves! If we have to use R.P.s—tiny, wedge-shaped brass nuts—as copperheads, at $6 a shot, we have to use them. We can use our R.P.s, stoppers, and hey, we can use our rivet loops, I bet."

"Yeah, Rich. I've already been doing that, and they work. You've got to mash the slide sleeve just right, but they work!"

"Good! So somehow we'll make it to Aquarian. Then we're up."

We felt a fresh commitment as we went to bed. Around 2:30 a.m. the drips started on Mark's face again. Jacket went back over head.

On July 6 Mark got us up pitch 11.

Wednesday, the 7th, we were up with the first light. I was determined to do pitch 12 in one day.

It looked like we had made the right choice to continue the climb, despite our pitiful copperhead tally. Mark's pitch had ended up as an A2 crack before the belay. So his pitch hadn't taken nearly the number of copperheads we had expected.

My pitch, however, although it started out as a crack, quickly turned into an arching, almost horizontal, seam. As I racked up that morning, I looked at the remains of our sad copperhead supply. I could see that I was going to be dependent upon pounding our 1/16-inch cable rivet loops into the seam. Fortunately, we had plenty of #0 heads, so I would try to find many places to use them. Our great lack was in the range of #2 heads and larger.

At 8:00 a.m. I stepped up onto the first placement of the pitch, a tied off baby angle.* As I progressed, the crack quickly turned into a seam. It was worse than I had expected it to be (what's new?), so once again I was looking at landing in the belay if anything pulled. At least this time there were no porties and only three haul bags to contend with. I was quite relieved to reach a short horizontal crack in which I could leap-frog our three #3 friends.

Strings of #0 heads later, it was early evening, but I had reached the end of the Overseer crack. The rock was bulged, and so it was poor for a hammock bivy where the seam ended. I planted a rivet out to the left on blank rock, to get the belay over onto flatter rock. From that rivet, I planted the first of four 1/4-inch bolts.

_____
*A small, half-inch thick piton.

The rock was slightly overhanging, and the exposure was tremendous. I wished for a 3/8-inch bolt. After drilling the anchor bolts, I anchored the ropes and prepared to haul. I yelled to Mark that he could clean the pitch.

Mark lowered out the haul bags and started the clean, somewhat unhappy at having to clean in the dark again. This was his second consecutive clean at night. When he got to the belay, he informed me that he had been keeping track of how many placements were in the pitch. It had taken 73 placements; most of them were #0 copperheads!

We settled into our hammocks at midnight after taking a short stock of our situation: all our drill bits were dull; the sharpening stone, which was a donut, was more hole than stone; our boot toes were wearing through again; my hammer head was loosening up again; we were completely out of #1, #2, #3, and #4 copperheads; and last but not least, we were down to two days of food each, even with reduced rations. We knew that we were at least four days from the rim!

To top it off, that night I dropped the shoulder spread-bar for my hammock. I couldn't believe it; I would have to finish the climb with rounded, scrunched shoulders every night.

We woke at dawn the next morning. My hands were trashed again. It seemed that I could put in one really long, merciless day then pay for it the next day!

I wanted to lead the last pitch of our route. Mark didn't want it. I couldn't lead, and we had things we needed to do all day without climbing.

The first order of the day was to eat. We decided to cut down to 1/4 rations, hoping not to go completely hungry for several days at the end. Our harnesses were already hanging loose on us, despite the fact that we had them cinched as tightly as they could go! We had been eating about 1,000 calories a day for a couple of days already, and this new reduction brought us down to 600 a day. We were learning what it was like to feel hungry all the time!

I ate a can of tuna, a can of peaches, and some gorp for breakfast: about 300 calories. I still felt hungry, and the day had hardly begun. We could eat only two meals a day to stay on our schedule, so I knew that our suffering would become acute.

We had saved some epoxy, so Mark went to work on his boots while I fixed my hammer again. I took another RURP, pounded it into the shaft as a wedge, bent it back and forth until it broke, and used the chisel to bury it, which seemed to tighten things up again. When my hammer was "fixed," I coated the toes of my boots with the last of our epoxy.

My hands really hurt after these activities, so Mark started sharpening drill bits while I sat around and looked at the position we occupied.

We were on the only vertical piece of rock around. The rock overhung and curved away from us in every direction. The effect was awesome! We felt like we were on the edge of a hot air balloon! The exposure was impressive from 1,600 feet in the air.

As the day passed, my hunger pangs became intense. We had been on slim rations for a while, but this was ridiculous!

Friday, July 9, found me drilling across the blankness toward Aquarian Wall. After many hooks and several rivets, I could swing over and peer down the dihedral into Aquarian Wall! Just below me was the thirteenth anchor: Coral Corner! What a break! I had Mark lower me a little farther, and I pulled around the edge of the big dihedral to clip a bolt. I quickly set up an anchor, asked Mark to lower the bags out to me, and then hauled them, while he cleaned the pitch. Our route was finished! Wings of Steel was finally up! Now just to rim out.

CHAPTER 13

The Summit?

When Mark arrived, we looked up at the fourteenth pitch: an overhanging slot filled with grass and weeds and pouring with water. While we were getting all the large crack gear out of the haul bag, I asked Mark if he had any interest in leading the pitch. A fruitless question. Of course he didn't! It was my day to lead.

It was even more disgusting than it looked. I had to use the pick end of my hammer to dig out huge piles of mud and grass from the slot so that I could reach way back into the crack and place a large friend, hex, or bong.

I had to wallow in the mud to dig for each placement, and torrents of green, textured slime flowed down the slot! Suddenly I understood the name "Aquarian." The route was definitely aquatic. Maybe it should have been named "Aquarium!"

Mark ducked into a small alcove at the belay, trying to avoid the falling mud, grass, and slime. However, he was only partially successful and got slime all over his shoulders and in his hair.

I was sickened as I climbed. The green slime was everywhere. As I continued the pitch, he had nothing better to do than watch the slime on the haul bags dry up. Suddenly he saw a white worm poke its head out of a nearby slime pack. The worm looked around and then moved from one part of the slime to the other. As it slithered across, Mark could see that it was two inches long and about as thick as a pencil lead.

Soon Mark saw other worms in the slime. Then many of them. They were everywhere! Mark was appalled. He had the good sense not to tell me that the slime was full of white worms. I don't know what I would have done if I had known.

As evening came, the slot ended, and conventional nailing led up to the fourteenth belay. I anchored myself in the dark, pulled out my headlamp, finished setting up the anchor, and prepared to haul. Mark cut the bags loose and started the clean, sickened as he had to wallow in the wormy slime, in the dark, by headlamp. I responded to his grumbling by pointing out that he could have led the pitch. I had offered! It was Mark's third consecutive nighttime clean.

Mark arrived at the belay just as I was anchoring the second bag. He clipped his aiders into the center of the four bolts and stood up on it. Suddenly Mark, I, and three haul bags dropped two feet into the night air!

The Leeper hanger on the old bolt had broken! We were caught by the other anchor bolts. We frantically looked here and there at the other three bolts. It was hard to see the big picture by headlamp in the dead of night!

I pulled back up to the anchor and placed a record-time bolt, with a dull bit, and the moment passed. Theoretically, the anchor was secure again. But the theory didn't make me feel any more secure! We had to hang in this place over the Sabbath.

After we got the anchor back together, Mark hauled the last bag up. Then, after changing our slime-sodden clothes, at 1:00 a.m. we finally could go to sleep.

Sabbath morning I realized that I was beginning to feel really weak from lack of calories. My hands were sore once again, and I was very happy it was the Sabbath. I would spend the day lying around, recuperating and trying to conserve energy.

For breakfast we were in for a treat. We were going to open Mark's last two-day food bundle and divide the contents. We knew that the food had to last until the rim, yet the sight of a small pile of food was going to look *very* good, even if we couldn't eat all of it at once. We opened the food bag and discovered a shocking surprise. One of Mark's tins of herring had split open at some point lower on the wall. The pungent, rotten, green contents had spread throughout Mark's two-day bundle.

We stared dismally at the mess for some time. We were going to starve! Then we started going through it to see what we could salvage. We had depended on that two-day bundle in our rationing schedule!

The rotten herrings had permeated everything that wasn't in a can! We started throwing granola bars, Figurines, dates, gorp, candy, etc. to the ground. It all had a green tinge and smelled awful. What a waste! We decided to clean up the cans before we ate anything from inside them. We couldn't risk eating a tiny chunk of the herring. We would do the cleanup at some later anchor, where we could really work on the cans.

Our food situation had gone from really grim, to downright desperate in one moment! My hunger pangs got even worse. The Sabbath came and went as just another 500-calorie day!

Sunday morning found Mark leading the fifteenth pitch of Aquarian, after a pitiful "breakfast." Break-fast? Ha! Seemed more like a continuation of the fast to us. We really wanted to get up the wall; we were getting weaker.

We spent the day getting up pitches fifteen and sixteen. The sixteenth pitch ended on a small ledge; not much, but it was the first ledge where we could lie down! What a break from the hammocks in which we had spent seven nights so far! Thirty-five days in portaledge or hammocks!

I cleaned up our herring-coated cans with surgical soap and water, and then after another ridiculously tiny meal, we settled down for the night. Mark tied his legs onto the ledge, because our legs overlapped to the thigh and his were on the outside. Although the ledge was a psychological break, our porties had actually been far more comfortable. Yet the ledge was better than our hammocks.

The fifteenth and sixteenth belays had been the first in seven days that were not on overhanging rock. The difficulty of the climb seemed to be lessening a little. Our main concern was to keep our energy levels high enough so that we could rim out.

On the morning of July 13 we got up at dawn and consolidated the items destined for the summit into two haul bags. Then we filled one haul bag with the last of our clothes, our rain gear, and some other miscellanies and tossed it off. The "rocket" had just lost another stage!

Mark started leading with mounting anticipation. We knew that we had to be close to Thanksgiving Ledge. We knew that on Thanksgiving we could traverse easily down to the West Buttress route, and from there it was only one pitch to the rim. We knew that we needed to get off this wall quickly. We were getting more debilitated by the working hour.

Unbelievably, around noon Mark reached Thanksgiving Ledge. This was a full day sooner than we had expected. Good thing, too, because we had looked at starving (that is, no food) that last day. Now it looked like we could have one last meal for breakfast the next day. Hopefully, that would get us to the rim.

Mark hauled our bags while I hiked up Thanksgiving Ledge to scout out the West Buttress route. When I returned, we divided loads, and began to hike up to the start of the last technical pitch we expected to do. By early evening we were poised to take off on the last pitch the first thing in the morning.

It was our thirty-eighth day from the ground. We watched the sun go down and retired. We were almost sad to be just about off the wall. We would miss the many special experiences. What would flat ground be like after so long? What would it be like to have all the food we wanted? What would it be like simply to walk, without having to worry about falling? What would a shower feel like? It was pretty unbelievable to think that we might actually get up this thing.

The next morning we awoke with the dawn. One can of fruit and a small can of tuna made a barely perceptible dent in my stomach. Mark had a can of fruit, some raisins, and six lemon drops. Our food supply was officially exhausted! We didn't have even one more lemon drop!

We remembered from a conversation with somebody that this last pitch was rated 5.9. I wondered what my problem was as I got more and more tired. It was supposed to be a simple finger jam,* but I struggled to get up it. *Is this 5.9? I must be really worn out from hunger!*

---

*Fingers are inserted into a think crack and turned to make them catch onto narrow spots so that you can pull up on them.

But I got up the pitch, anchored the ropes, and hauled the bags. Mark was soon up with me, and we were at the top of the supposed final pitch. We looked up but still couldn't see the rim. All we found was just a low angled face, leading up to a bushy gully. *Well, the rim must be above the gully*, I thought.

But getting into the gully revealed no summit either, only another steep headwall. Mark and I paddled up the 5.4 headwall and were dismayed to see more steep terraces. Where *was* the summit? We were weakening rapidly! We had left the haul bags at the top of the 5.9 pitch, so at least we weren't dealing with their weight.

We hiked and scrambled up the terraces for half an hour. Then, slowly but surely, the terrain began to round off to horizontal, and after pulling ourselves up over a boulder, we could see the rounded summit dome.

Panting, we collapsed by a pine tree. It was 1:00 p.m. We had finally reached the summit! There was no "rim," only El Cap's shoulder rounding off to horizontal. We lay around under a tree for about half an hour as we tried to recuperate. We were wiped out! How were we going to get our gear to the top and down the trail? It was eight and a half miles back to the valley floor. Did we even have the energy to make it down the trail, much less get our bags out too? We had about 200 pounds down there somewhere!

Just as we were discussing what to do, two young male tourists came into view over the summit dome. They had day packs on their backs, which to our view had giant, blinking neon signs spelling the word FOOD!

We hauled ourselves to our feet and approached them, well aware that we looked pathetic!

After a little negotiation, they agreed to trade us a couple of sandwiches for some of our water.

After eating, Mark volunteered to go back down to our haul bags and get our sleeping gear so that we could just leave the bags where they were and hike out. We would return later when we were in better shape.

After an hour, Mark returned with our sleeping gear, and we

prepared to hike out. Since there was only the one 25-pound pack to carry, we decided to each carry it out halfway. I would start because I had been resting most recently. I threw the thing on, and we hiked over the summit dome toward the Yosemite Falls trail.

As the hours passed, the only things that kept us going were prayer and the thoughts of the unlimited food in the valley. We switched the pack at the halfway point.

While passing through the forest, we thought about how strange it was to walk uninhibited, to be able to see trees and moss and ferns and to walk on dirt. Living things were everywhere, and soon we would eat!

At about 6:00 p.m., we straggled into Camp 4. It looked so strange: people, colors, smells, and cars in abundance. Civilization! We paused—we didn't know for sure if we liked this! The wall had been scary, but clean and peaceful. This campground was a mess! Well, we would sort that out later. On to the phones!

We made some quick phone calls, telling people that we had made it. Then we hopped the shuttle to Camp Curry, walked up to the takeout window, and ordered ice cream Frosties with the last of our money. They were indescribable!

The next day we hiked up to the base and cleaned up all the garbage. When I say "all," I mean all! There wasn't even a cigarette butt on the ground at the base when we left. We cleaned from Aquarian Wall down to Cosmos. We collected five 55-gallon garbage bags full, though half of the bulk wasn't even our own garbage.

On July 25 we hiked again to the base of our climb. After repeating the bogus start to the second anchor, we rappelled, replacing the bolts and rivets in the original first two pitches as we went. We figured that if it could be chopped at night on jumars, we could replace it on rappel. After all, we had already climbed it; they had never climbed it! So the original start was back up in its original state.

On the evening of the twenty-sixth, we packed the car and drove out of the valley. At 2:30, on the morning of July 27, we crested the Grapevine and looked down at the lights of Los Angeles. It was over! Or so we thought.

Epilogue

O n our fourth night off of the wall, Richard Jensen and I
were sleeping in a large dome tent, the ceiling of which
resembled our portaledge rain flies. We were both asleep
when a tinkling noise began, which sounded like a wind chime.
Richard woke up, and hearing what he thought was a falling object,
curled up into a tight ball to reduce surface area. He yelled at me
to wake up. I, too, curled up into a tight shivering ball. Richard
blurted out, 'What is it? What's falling?' I responded, 'It sounds like
someone dropped their pin rack.' The thought of 50 miniature
missiles hurtling down the wall had us both in horror. Immediately,
I was concerned about the strength of our anchor, especially as I
couldn't remember what it was. My mind blanked out. What was
our anchor? 'What does our anchor consist of?' I demanded. A long
pause followed as we strained to conjure up what was holding us
to the wall. Then Richard responded, 'We don't have an anchor.' I
thought, *You dummy. We've got to have an anchor.* Then a second
later it hit me. *We were on the ground.*

"The next morning I began to wonder what had happened to
our minds. Just exactly what impact had living for 39 consecutive
days and nights on El Capitan doing our first ascent, Wings of Steel,
had on us? I thought back to the conception of the climb and was
boggled by what had transpired since. It all started so innocently."

Yes, the climb started so innocently. However, our innocence is
gone. Many years have passed since we climbed Wings of Steel. We
know of at least seven attempts to climb the route, including two
attempts by parties with an "ax to grind." None of those teams was
able to complete successfully even the first pitch.

One of these efforts was made by two men, one of whom was

involved in chopping our first two pitches in 1982. This man, who claimed, "My grandmother could do that route," was unable to ascend more than 60 feet of the first pitch. Later his partner told us that he had hung "screaming in terror," trying to figure out how to get himself out of his position.

After Wings of Steel, as we went to various other climbing areas, the controversy continued. Some people were for us, others against us. Often the discussions about the route became quite heated. It seemed that our route had become a catalyst to unleash the undercurrent of strong feelings from people on both sides of the ethical debate. Two camps formed: those who supported the chopping party as heroes who were doing what had to be done to keep the standards high, and those who supported our route as an example of people's right to climb for their own reasons.

In efforts to lighten the situation a little, Mark and I had some shirts made up that said, "BOLT MASTER, WINGS OF STEEL" and "WINGS OF STEEL, DRILL FIRST, THINK LATER." For some, this approach worked. For others, the shirts were only a further outrage.

Years passed, and things calmed down. During the summer of 1987, Mark and I climbed the Sea of Dreams on El Capitan. At the time, and in many people's minds even now, the Sea was regarded as the hardest big wall climb in the world. This earned us the "credibility" in the climbing community that was deemed so important when we did Wings of Steel. We did not find the Sea to be as consistently difficult or mentally traumatic as we had found Wings of Steel to be. We also found that large amounts of drilling were used as the first ascent team established the route—a fact that we did not know when we were being indicted because of our "drilling ethic."

In September of 1988 Rob Slater, a well-known veteran of hideous valley walls, and Bruce Hunter headed up Wings of Steel. After fixing the first two pitches, they spent two days and one night on the climb, reaching the fifth pitch anchor. The ascent was going well, yet after two days in the kind of intense heat that Mark and I had feared we would encounter but didn't, they decided to retreat from what was like a reflector oven.

I spoke with Rob on the phone as this book was going to press. I wanted his impressions of the climb. He said, "There's a lot of drilling, but there's a lot of really delicate hooking too. Especially the second pitch was very well done. The route contains the most technical hooking I've ever seen. The hooking is way harder than on the other 'hard' routes in the valley, like Lost in America or the Sea of Dreams."

I'm sorry that Rob and Bruce got hit with the heat. Rob is someone I would have liked to see get the second ascent.

Some of our former worst critics apologized for their role in the controversy. One member of the chopping party even apologized. We held no grudges. We had gotten what we wanted from the route. The years had calmed our anger at the many abuses we had endured.

Outside magazine ran an article about climbing ethics, and the "Wings of Steel Syndrome" was coined, referring to attempts to enforce local climbing area ethics. During the years attitudes have changed, and the climbing community now generally frowns upon enforcement of ethical opinions.

At the present, Mark has graduated from college and is a math and physics teacher at Orangewood Academy in California. I'm back in school, soon to finish my degree in philosophy at Cal State San Bernardino, also in California.

Since the Sea, Mark and I have climbed El Cap twice more together, and once each solo. Each time I go climbing, there are hardships to endure and difficulties to overcome. But no climbing experience has even approached the intensity of those 39 days and nights in 1982 when Mark and I were living in the sky.

Excerpt from "Wings of Steel: Living in the Sky," by Mark A. Smith. Published in the June 1983 issue of *Climbing Magazine.*

Appendix

I will now attempt to explain where all our hauling weight came from—all 1,100 pounds of it!

FOOD LIST
250 pounds

I will give Mark's food list only, because we took up virtually the same things, and identically the same weight. Our food haul bags weighed 125 pounds each.

8 cans fried chicken[1]	5 tins herring
4 cans tuna (large)	16 cans tuna (small)
6 cans Vienna sausage	10 cans chicken
10 cans Vienna chicken	2 pkgs. beef jerky
5 cans cranberry sauce	5 cans applesauce
15 cans peaches	5 cans fruit cocktail
5 cans apricots	3 pkgs. dried fruit
3 pounds dates	10 boxes raisins (small)
4 cans olives (large)	3 cans asparagus
3 cans peas	3 cans mixed vegetables
6 cans spinach	3 cans olives (small)
12 pkgs. Pop-Tarts	24 pkgs. Figurines
24 packets granola bars	8 tins pudding
2 pkgs. coated nuts	3 pkgs. almonds
2 pkgs. red vines	1 pkg. red twists
4 packs bubble gum	1 bag lemon drops

There was one major difference in our food lists. I am a vegetarian, and Mark was not (he now is). So I substituted Loma

Linda Foods Fried Chicken and Linketts (a hot dog substitute) in place of Mark's meat items. I also chose not to include any vegetable cans and substituted fruit in their place. We both brought up pounds of candy of all types, mostly chocolate and licorice.

WATER
450 Pounds

We brought up 200 liters of water because we were expecting searing June and July temperatures, which never came. We knew that we couldn't endure dehydration in the usual 100+ degree temperatures. Two haul bags contained 145 pounds of water. One bag had only 115 pounds of water in it. Then there was the weight of the bags and bottles.

PERSONAL GEAR
150 Pounds

A single haul bag contained our sleeping systems, clothes, and personal miscellanies. Our sleeping gear included our portaledges, rain flies, extenders, hammocks, sleeping bags, and Ensolite brand pads. Mark also brought up a bivy bag. For clothing we brought everything from pants to socks in just enough quantity to make it a month without wearing encrusted items too long. Our miscellaneous items included everything from headlamps to first-aid kits.

CLIMBING GEAR
250 Pounds

Our philosophy with the gear, since we didn't know for sure what we would find up there, was to err on the side of hauling something we didn't need, rather than to need something we hadn't hauled. We realized that we could only take this so far, however. All the gear that wasn't in use stayed in this last haul bag.

9 ropes (11 mm x 165')   1 rope (7 mm x 165')
1 rope (9 mm x 165')   180 carabiners
13 friends (#1-#4)   30 hexentrics (#3-#11)
60 stoppers (#1-#10)   2 climbing harnesses
2 pairs of E.B. climbing shoes   ? slings (1 ½' dia.)
150¼" x 1¼" Rawl bolts   200 rivets (¼ x ¾"
35⅜" x 2½" Rawl drive bolts   ? Star crown-head bolts
250 Leeper bolt hangers   18 assorted drill bits
50 Rurps   40 knifeblade pitons
40 angles (½" to 1½")   20 bongs (2" to 5")
2 drill holders   2 crag hammers
1 ball peen hammer (back-up)   100 1" tubular webbing
5 Leeper narrow hooks   100 ⁹⁄₁₆" webbing slings
4 Leeper broad hooks   10 five-step aiders
3 Chouinard cliff hanger hooks   50 assorted lost arrows
? spare 1" tublar webbing   ? spare ⁹⁄₁₆" webbing
15 Leeper "Z" pins   12 SMC shallow angles
5 padded gear slings   2 locking carabiners
20 feet of 2" web (for swamies) 500 copperheads (#00-#4)[2]

Obviously, this is not an inclusive list of what went up. There
are all kinds of items I'm sure I have missed. For example, our five
rolls of one-inch adhesive tape. But you can get an idea of how we
managed to rack up 1,100 pounds. When Mark's and my weight is
added, the total weight on the first bivy anchor was well in excess
of 1,400 pounds.

DRILLING AND OTHER TRIVIA

There were 113 drilled placements in the slab by ascending the
Bogus Start. However, an additional 20 drilled placements must be
added when you include the original start. So there are a grand
total of 133 drilled placements in the slab. Of that number, 78 were
rivets.

There were a total of 145 holes drilled to do the route. However, by including the (now replaced) original start, the total tally comes to 165 total drilled placements. Of that number, 41 bolts were for anchors.

We used 151 hooks to ascend the route. All but five were Leeper narrows. We placed 205 copperheads, most of which were #0, #1, and #2.

We hauled 92 sack pitches, with an average sack weight of 110 pounds. The average hauling pitch was 110 feet. This amounts to more than a million foot-pounds of effort expended.

---

[1] Loma Linda Foods imitation meat

[2] We were unable to place a single #00 copperhead in the route. The #00's made up $1/4$ of our total heads.